THE LUTHERAN STUDY BIBLE
Journal

Life by His Word

CONCORDIA PUBLISHING HOUSE • SAINT LOUIS

Copyright © 2009 Concordia Publishing House
3558 S. Jefferson Avenue, St. Louis, MO 63118-3968
1-800-325-3040 • www.cph.org

All rights reserved. Unless specifically noted, no part of this publication may
be reproduced, stored in a retrieval system, or transmitted, in any form or by
any means, electronic, mechanical, photocopying, recording, or otherwise,
without the prior written permission of Concordia Publishing House.

Cover photos: © iStockphoto.com
Illustration: © shutterstock.com

The two-year reading plan, application notes, prayers, and topical index
are adapted from *The Lutheran Study Bible*. Copyright © 2009 Concordia
Publishing House. All rights reserved.

Scripture quotations from the ESV Bible® (The Holy Bible, English Standard
Version®), copyright ©2001 by Crossway Bibles, a publishing ministry of
Good News Publishers. Used by permission. All rights reserved.

Hymn texts with the abbreviation *LSB* are from *Lutheran Service Book*,
copyright © 2006 Concordia Publishing House. All rights reserved.

The quotations from the Lutheran Confessions in the publication are from
Concordia: The Lutheran Confessions, second edition; edited by Paul McCain,
et al., copyright © 2006 Concordia Publishing House. All rights reserved.

Manufactured in the United States of America

1 2 3 4 5 6 7 8 9 10   18 17 16 15 14 13 12 11 10 09

❖ ❖ ❖

Using Your Journal

Through Holy Scripture God answers essential questions about life on earth, death, and life everlasting. God works through the Scriptures to make you aware of your sins, to call you to repentance, to announce that His Son has taken away your sins, and to show you the path of life. Let this journal be your guide and tool for further understanding.

Read, prayerfully. Each day begin with prayer, asking the Holy Spirit to open your heart, mind, and soul to what He wants you to understand and to know from your reading of Scripture. Read the selected Scripture passage. The reading plan will lead you through the whole Bible in two years (if you read a passage six days each week). Or you can break the readings into smaller sections and move at your own pace and comfort level. If a word or phrase intimidates or frustrates you, use your study Bible's notes and articles for additional insight.

Reflect, prayerfully. Ponder the words of the Scripture reading through prayer, as you reflect back to God the words He has given to you. Your journal pages give you ample space to write your thoughts. You do not have to use every line; just record your reflections. You may choose to write about a particular verse: your personal insights, what you already know about this verse, or what you want to learn more about. You may choose to write about your day or your feelings. You may choose to list prayer requests. However you decide to use this space, do so prayerfully, trusting that God always knows what is in your heart.

Review, prayerfully. At the bottom of each journal page is an excerpt from *The Lutheran Study Bible*. These notes provide a summary of the daily reading. Each note points to your great need for a Savior, and the fulfillment of God's promises in the person of Jesus Christ. When you feel overwhelmed by sin or the trials of the day, these notes will return your focus to Christ—the source of your salvation.

Conclude with a final prayer. A brief prayer concludes each journal page. Use these as a guide for your personal prayer. The inside front and back covers of *The Lutheran Study Bible* offer additional prayers.

As you continue prayerfully to read, reflect, and review, you will see how the stories in Scripture weave together to point to Christ and our salvation in Him and how they speak to you, in your life, right now. The **Personal Index** offers an additional tool to help you see this tapestry. As you journal, you will encounter Scripture passages or write journal entries that you will want to reference again. Record these references in your index—under an existing heading or your own, which you can add in the space provided. Beneath

> ENCOURAGEMENT
> Ps 91; Col 4:2–6
> *Heb 10:19–15; p. 47*

PERSONAL INDEX SAMPLE

each topic is a reference to lead you to answers and comfort in God's Word. To make it easier to reference specific Scripture passages or your thoughts on a specific topic, each page of your journal is numbered.

However and whenever you choose to use this journal, my prayer is that you will develop a consistent, personal time with God through prayerful meditation on His Word, and learn to "take every thought captive to obey Christ" (2 Corinthians 10:5).

Laura L. Lane, Editor

God makes all things good. Indeed, God even used His creation to accomplish our salvation: a cross made of wood; the water of Baptism; the bread and wine of the Eucharist; the printed words on the page in, with, and under which He reveals His Word of life to us.

✤ **Preserve me and Your creation, O Lord, by Your grace. Amen.**

DATE

TOPICS

Genesis 3:1–24

We have received God's grace through the Seed of the woman, and now we are sent out to the ends of the earth to bear witness to the completion of God's plan of redemption and to offer His grace in Jesus Christ to all the descendants of Adam and Eve.

❖ **O Savior, write our names into Your story, into the Lamb's Book of Life. Amen.**

_____

_____

_____

_____

_____

_____

_____

_____

_____

_____

_____

_____

_____

_____

_____

_____

_____

_____

_____

_____

God's patience is about to give way to judgment. But God also plans to have mercy. Even as Noah finds favor in the eyes of the Lord, so also the faithful of all times have God's favor on account of the promised Savior.

✤   **We thank You, O Lord, that You look upon us with favor because of Christ Jesus, our Savior. Keep us ever in this faith. Amen.**

All Christians experience turbulence in their lives that can lead them to the brink of despair. But through Noah, God has demonstrated that He will lift up and save His faithful people whom He has cleansed in Holy Baptism.

✛   **Lord, give to Your people today the confidence in Your salvation. Amen.**

God is faithful to His covenants, even when people are not. The message of every rainbow tells us He is faithful to His promise to provide a Savior.

❖   **O God, for Jesus' sake, grant that every sighting of a rainbow may bring to mind Your promises of grace and mercy. Amen.**

DATE

TOPICS

God's Spirit works faith, when and where He pleases, through the Word. He made Abram into a great nation, blessing all the world through the Son. As Abram's offspring by faith, we have the blessing of God's forgiveness and life without end.

✤ **Heavenly Father, call us to cling to everything You command and to live by the blessing of Your Word. Amen.**

We often find ourselves in circumstances that show the opposite of what God says. Abram went forth—out of the land of promise—trusting that God would fulfill His Word. In the fullness of time, God brought forth the Son by whom all nations would be blessed.

✣   **Lord God, when everything appears to contradict what You have promised, teach us to rely on Your unfailing Word. Amen.**

Rest in God's promises given to you in Jesus and delivered to you in His Word and Sacraments. They are enough, because Jesus was enough.

✤ **Dear Father, rescue us from our enemies by Your promise made sure in Your Son, who delivers our inheritance to us in the New Testament of His blood. In Jesus' name. Amen.**

How often our own households and marriages are torn asunder when we devise ways and means that God has not commanded! Consider how our Lord submitted Himself to the Father's will, suffering at the hands of evil men and dying in their place. He has seen your suffering, and has taken it upon Himself.

✤ **Dear Lord, work among us by Your means of grace, exercising Your fatherly care. Amen.**

The evils of Sodom remind us of our own time, with evil that also cries out for divine intervention. Intercede in prayer for those who have not yet repented of their wickedness. Take comfort in the truth that God spares the wicked for the sake of one righteous man—Jesus Christ.

✣ **O Lord, spare us who live in this world of wickedness, for Jesus' sake. Amen.**

How impatient we can become when things do not go as we think they should. But God is faithful, even when our patience and faith fall short. He has delivered the greatest of His promises, to give salvation and everlasting life to all who believe in the Lord Jesus.

✤ **Heavenly Father, keep us patient and faithful while You carry out Your plan for our lives and our salvation. Amen.**

DATE

TOPICS

Often we fail tests of faith that do not begin to compare to Abraham's. Thankfully, there was an even greater sacrifice when God the Father in heaven offered the sacrifice of His beloved Son to secure forgiveness for our failures.

✣ **Lamb of God, You take away the sin of the world; have mercy on us. Amen.**

Many people wrongly see romance and emotion as the basis of marriage. Instead, God wants marriage (lifelong faithfulness vowed publicly) to be the basis for the love of husband and wife. Such love is a picture of Christ's love for the Church.

❖ **O Christ, our heavenly Bridegroom, help us to trust the Word spoken by Your servants, the Word that calls us to be joined to You. Amen.**

Esau disdains his birthright, and Jacob schemes against his brother. By our sinful nature and our actions, we are unworthy of any blessing of this life, especially the gift of forgiveness and eternal life with Christ. Yet, in His mercy, we receive a great inheritance because Christ has made us a part of His family in Baptism.

❖   **Praise be to our Savior, who has granted us an inheritance among the saints! Amen.**

_____

_____

_____

_____

_____

_____

_____

_____

_____

_____

_____

_____

_____

_____

_____

_____

_____

_____

_____

_____

Our hope cannot rest on human nature or accomplishments. Despite this sorry state, Christ loved us and gave Himself up for us, a fragrant offering and sacrifice to God. He was cursed so we may be blessed (Galatians 3:13).

✣ **Lord, we thank You for providing a salvation that does not rely on our virtue or accomplishments. Amen.**

In business, you will be tempted to act dishonestly, as Laban did. Instead, pray for wisdom and shrewdness. Remember that the Lord gives us the blessings of His cross in Word and Sacraments and will set all things right at His second coming.

✢ **Come, Lord Jesus, and grant us Your wholesome wisdom. Amen.**

Alone and faced with danger, Jacob finds God to be his adversary. It does not always seem that God is on our side. Sometimes He causes Christians to bear trials, temptations, and suffering not to destroy us but to strengthen us and finally bless us. Christian faith clings to God's Word of mercy in Jesus Christ.

✣ **Lord, in Baptism, You have promised to be my God. Grant to me what You see that I need. Amen.**

Those who receive God's promises, such as Rachel and Isaac, are still subject to death. Mourning is a part of life in a sin-broken world. When sorrows surround you, call on the Lord in prayer. Remember and celebrate His promises. Because Jesus conquered death and sin, we have comfort in the midst of all troubles.

✤ **O Lord, forgive our sins, and bring us to eternal life for Jesus' sake. Amen.**

Joseph is favored by his father but hated by his brothers. Those who love virtue will be hated and envied by the wicked. Yet we should also pursue humility and avoid arrogance. Thanks be to God, His favored Son died to redeem His people, though they hated Him. In righteous humility, He redeemed us too.

✣ **Almighty God bless us with the healing love of Your Son, Jesus. Amen.**

Today, pursue chastity and flee fornication, as Joseph did. Mark and avoid the bad example of Potiphar's wife, who slandered Joseph. Take comfort: whenever the Lord places the cross and suffering on His people, He also gives consolation and help.

✚ **Lord Jesus Christ, be with us in our temptations, free us from the prison of sin, and by Your cross bring us to eternal life. Amen.**

Once people are free from danger or troubling situations, they so easily forget those who helped them, and they neglect to honor God, who delivered them. Although others may forget us, even if our father and mother forsake us, the Lord will take care of His people and remember them in His mercy (Psalm 27:10).

✤ **Lord God, remember us in mercy for the sake of Your Son, Jesus Christ, our Lord. Amen.**

The devil's tools—fortune-tellers and sorcerers—are powerless in divine matters. Like Joseph, we should praise God for any good thing we have. The best thing we have is God Himself—speaking to us through His Word, redeeming us through His Son, and bringing us to Himself through His Sacraments and Spirit.

✤ **O Lord, we praise You for Your mercy, through Jesus Christ, our Lord. Amen.**

In hard times, those who have should share with those who have not. After long periods of suffering, at just the right time, the Lord will give help to His people, just as He did for Joseph. Through His Son, Jesus, God rules over us and gives us what we need: pardon, provision, and peace.

❖ **Heavenly Father, give us this day our daily bread, and deliver us from evil, for Jesus' sake. Amen.**

God reminds us to humbly acknowledge and take responsibility for our sin. When Judah shows himself willing to be enslaved in place of his brother, this prefigures the saving work of his descendant, Jesus, who gave Himself as mediator, ransom, and sacrifice for the world.

✤   **Jesus, turn us from sin, selfishness, and alienation to live for You, as You have died for us. Amen.**

God rules the world and brings evil to a good end for the sake of His people, as He did with Joseph's slavery. Let us hold fast to the mercy and doctrine that God has revealed. In Christ, our sin is forgiven, and God gives us the joy of reconciliation and new life.

✤ **Lord Jesus, give us the benefits of Your death, and form our lives to Your cross. Amen.**

Like Joseph, we must learn not to value human convention over God's Word and purposes. As Jacob adopted Ephraim and Manasseh, God has graciously adopted us in Holy Baptism (Galatians 3:27–4:7).

✤   **"Restore us, O God; let Your face shine, that we may be saved!" (Psalm 80:3). Amen.**

_____

_____

_____

_____

_____

_____

_____

_____

_____

_____

_____

_____

_____

_____

_____

_____

_____

_____

_____

_____

_____

_____

Joseph's life illustrates one of God's promises for obedience to the Law—prosperous, long life (Exodus 20:12). The coming gift is the Lord Himself, His visitation, fulfilled in part in the exodus from Egypt, though that pales before God's final visitation in the Messiah (Luke 1:68).

✤   **Give us hearts that long for Your return to lead us out of the Egypt of this world to Yourself in heaven. Amen.**

Israel emerges as a people. God's blessing and the fulfillment of God's promise gives growth and preserves His people in a foreign land. God blesses us as He blessed Israel, yet He has also revealed to us His greatest blessings in His only-begotten Son.

✣　**O Lord, the multitude of Your blessings leads us to multiply thanks and praise to Your name. Amen.**

God does not forget Israel but remembers His covenant with their fathers. In Holy Communion, we remember God's new covenant in Christ. Holy Communion is God's promise of forgiveness to us and assures us that He will never forget us.

✠ **Rescue us, dearest Jesus, from the slavery of sin, and deliver us to the Promised Land. Amen.**

Like Moses, we Christians have been called to speak God's Word. This is an important assignment because it is through the Word that God "works in people's hearts true repentance, knowledge of sins, and true faith in God's Son, Jesus Christ" (FC SD II 50).

✤ **Lord, bless my mouth that I may speak Your Word clearly and with sincerity. Amen.**

As a Levite, Moses has good family connections, but this does not translate into an eager willingness to serve the Lord. How different is another Servant of the Lord with good family! Jesus' willing obedience frees us from the eternal consequences of our sinful fears, doubts, and stubbornness.

✤   **Dear Father in heaven, I praise You for Your victory in Christ, who paid our ransom with His life. Amen.**

The Lord begins to deliver His people from Egypt through water, by which He will later destroy Pharaoh's army and set Israel apart. Today, praise God, who has likewise delivered you through a water miracle: Holy Baptism.

✢ **Dear Father in heaven, guard us from the craftiness of the devil, who would seek to undo us and draw us away from Christ. Amen.**

The plague of gnats is more intense than the previous plagues. People who trust Christ the Lord are drawn closer to Him in times of tribulation, seeking His forgiveness, comfort, strength, and healing for the sake of His cross and resurrection.

✢ **In Christ Jesus, daily increase our faith that we may recognize Your loving hand at work in our lives. Amen.**

The Egyptians would soon be exposed to the testimony that the Lord is patient and slow to anger, but at the proper time, judgment will come. Thanks be to God that by the vicarious sacrifice of Jesus Christ, we are His children through Holy Baptism, protected from the final judgment.

❖ **O Lord, be gracious and merciful for Jesus' sake. Amen.**

_____

_____

_____

_____

_____

_____

_____

_____

_____

_____

_____

_____

_____

_____

_____

_____

_____

_____

_____

_____

_____

_____

Passover marks a new era for the people of Israel and foreshadows the new, spiritual Israel in Christ, the perfect Lamb who takes away the sin of the world (1 Corinthians 5:7; Hebrews 7:27).

✜   O Lord, You are the Good Shepherd, who seeks and saves the lost. Save me, O Lamb of God, who takes away the sin of the world. Amen.

The Lord sets Israel apart by instituting observances that help them remember their freedom won in the exodus. Jesus offered Himself as the perfect, "once for all" sacrifice (Hebrews 10:10). He purifies us from our sin and consecrates us so that God can call us His own.

✤ **Lord, I praise and thank You for giving me a new start! Amen.**

_____

_____

_____

_____

_____

_____

_____

_____

_____

_____

_____

_____

_____

_____

_____

_____

_____

_____

_____

_____

_____

_____

When Israel crosses through the sea, they leave behind slavery and a future of death in Egypt for freedom and a future of life with God. God has intervened for us in Baptism (1 Corinthians 10:1–2), saving us from our old slavery in sin and bringing us into the new freedom of the Gospel.

✛   "The Lᴏʀᴅ is my strength and my song, and He has become my salvation" (Exodus 15:2). Amen.

The Lord patiently supplies Israel with drinking water. Without water, there is no life. And if we go without spiritual refreshment, we will die eternally. However, God meets this spiritual need for us just as certainly as He slaked Israel's thirst at Marah.

✣   **Jesus Christ, Living Water, refresh us in this wilderness. Amen.**

When Israel runs out of water, they grumble instead of turning to God, their Rock, for help. God in His graciousness furnishes the water they desperately need. He was stricken Himself for what they deserve. Christ Jesus is the Rock of Israel and our Rock of salvation.

✤   **O Lord, our Rock, give us the stability, refuge, and living water that we need. Amen.**

DATE

TOPICS

Moses serves as chief mediator between God and the Israelites. This role of Moses foreshadowed Jesus, our mediator with the Father. God has revealed Himself in Jesus for all to see, and through Jesus we may approach God as one of His own children.

❖ **Jesus Christ, judge and guide us so we may be Your faithful servants who minister in Your name. Amen.**

Sinfulness prevents the people from approaching God personally. Yet God graciously appoints an intermediary, Moses, through whom He makes His covenant with His people. Thanks be to God, we can approach Him with confidence through our mediator, Jesus.

✤ **O Lord, deliver and consecrate us this day in the renewal of our Baptism, that we may lead lives that honor You. Amen.**

Because we, God's people, continue to sin, even though we are justified by faith, we need God's Law as a guide in life. All people are sinners, and our gracious Lord makes His forgiveness available to all.

✤   "[God] breaks the pow'r of canceled sin; He sets the pris'ner free. His blood can make the foulest clean; His blood avails for me." Amen. (*LSB* 528:4)

Sin creates an impassible barrier between God and people. By the blood of the covenant, the Lord anticipates the forgiveness of sins in Jesus, who would become "sin" for us in order to redeem us (2 Corinthians 5:21).

❖ **"Purge me with hyssop, and I shall be clean; wash me, and I shall be whiter than snow" (Psalm 51:7). Amen.**

Specific limits mark the holiness of the Lord, limiting the approach of humans to Him. Due to our sins, we cannot approach the Holy One of Israel and live. Through Christ's work on the cross, we have access to the court, the Most Holy Place in heaven (cf Hebrews 4:14).

✤ **Jesus, may Your Spirit lead us to confess Your loving mercy. Amen.**

The Lord required that even the clothing and movement of the high priest would bring glory and offer praise. Reassess your offering of praise and service to the Lord. Give all glory to Jesus, who diligently bore your guilt and consecrates you by grace.

✢ **O Lord God, draw us to the One whom our pastors preach, Christ crucified for the forgiveness of sins. Amen.**

Without faith, it is impossible for us to pray rightly and to please God (Hebrews 11:6). Jesus' life and work was pleasing incense before His Father. Through Jesus' intercession, our prayers are acceptable.

✤ **May the Good News impel us to intercede continually before You, Jesus, on behalf of the Church and for the needs of all people. Amen.**

We may grow impatient or doubt God's promises. In fear or doubt, we may turn to idols of our own: anything that we "fear, love, and trust" more than the true God. But Jesus Christ alone is able to take the sin of the world upon Himself and give us His perfect righteousness.

✜ **O Christ, forgive my sins, and strengthen me to believe in You and love You. Amen.**

Moses receives an extraordinary gift: God speaks to him face-to-face, as to a friend. Jesus Christ gives believers in the New Testament the same gift. He says, "I have called you friends, for all that I have heard from My Father I have made known to you" (John 15:15).

✤   **Thank You, Jesus, for being my friend. May I always hear Your voice in faith. Amen.**

If left up to us, we could not live in God's covenant. Here, in the middle of the worship provisions of the covenant, God foreshadows His solution: redemption through sacrifice (v. 20). The Lamb of God died for us that we might live.

✤ **Lord Jesus, Lamb of God, I am grateful for Your sacrifice. Strengthen me by Your Spirit to worship You properly. Amen.**

God calls the people again to share in His Sabbath rest. The soul that forsakes the gift of Sabbath rest remains in torment. Our true rest is in the one true God, who grants life, peace, and all blessings.

✣   **We thank You, Jesus, for patiently having had mercy on us, that we can rest in the work of salvation that You have accomplished for us. Amen.**

Jesus compares the tabernacle and Herod's temple with the temple of His body (Matthew 27:40; John 2:19–22), by which we have full remission of sin. By the temple of Jesus' body, we approach the Father.

✣   **Lord Jesus, we praise You that the prophecies of the Old Testament (Luke 24:27) have been fulfilled in Your life, death, and resurrection. Amen.**

DATE

TOPICS

The priestly garments are completed. Just as the garments of the priests set them apart, so the Lord clothes us with His righteousness and sets us apart as a royal priesthood.

✤ **Bless me, O Savior, and consecrate me for service in Your kingdom. Amen.**

_____

_____

_____

_____

_____

_____

_____

_____

_____

_____

_____

_____

_____

_____

_____

_____

_____

_____

_____

_____

_____

Today, just as the Israelites faithfully confessed their sins and prayed to the Lord, present your confession of sins and prayers of repentance and faith before Him in the name of "the Lamb of God, who takes away the sin of the world!" (John 1:29).

✤   **Almighty Father, may we always rejoice in Your abundant grace, through Christ, our Lord. Amen.**

Peace offerings acknowledge God's grace toward His people. Jesus' death was God's great peace offering for the world, since the Father brought about our peace and reconciliation through Jesus.

✣   **Gracious Father, we thank You for Your peace through Christ, who offered Himself for the sins of the world. Grant us generous hearts to share Your peace. Amen.**

_____

_____

_____

_____

_____

_____

_____

_____

_____

_____

_____

_____

_____

_____

_____

_____

_____

God would have fellowship with His people only after they atoned for sin through sacrifice. Christ's body was offered as a sin offering and a reparation offering to God. By Christ's holy flesh and blood, God keeps His people holy (Hebrews 10:10).

✢   **Father in heaven, we thank You for Your surpassing gifts of grace and fellowship, which come through Christ's atoning sacrifice. Amen.**

In the Divine Service, God's people today share much in common with God's Old Testament people. Like them, we come before God and humbly confess our sins. We also seek anew the promise of forgiveness offered by God's grace.

✤   **Precious Lord, we thank You for the glimpse of salvation in the sacrifices offered by Your Old Testament priests. Amen.**

_____

_____

_____

_____

_____

_____

_____

_____

_____

_____

_____

_____

_____

_____

_____

_____

_____

_____

_____

_____

_____

The story of Nadab and Abihu's thoughtlessness shows us that God is present in grace and in wrath. Jesus Christ, who bore the sins of all, declares us acceptable to God (1 Peter 2:24). Scripture calls this justification.

✤   **Lord, thank You for Your grace, which justified sinners like us and made us holy through the body and blood of Your Son, Jesus Christ. Amen.**

In His mercy, God provides His priests with purification rites to cleanse individuals and homes. Ultimately, God sent His Son to enter the unclean home of sinners (cf. Matthew 26:6). Christ purifies and blesses our homes by His presence, as we pray, "Come, Lord Jesus, be our guest, and let these gifts to us be blessed."

✢ **Bless our homes, Lord, we pray. Amen.**

God proclaims His dwelling place as the exclusive place for sacrifices. He does not want His people running after false gods. Today, avoid every association with idolatrous practices. Jesus is the only way to the Father (John 1:17–18; 14:6).

❖ **Father in heaven, grant us undivided hearts focused on Your dear Son. Amen.**

TOPICS

The Gospel sets people free from sin, but that freedom is not an excuse for committing sin. God knows our hearts and provides marriage to protect us from sin (1 Corinthians 7:2). In faithfulness to His Church, He hallows us and provides for our forgiveness from all sins.

❖ **Lord of the Church, forgive me and protect my heart from all impurity. Amen.**

Recognize that God made His people holy by grace, and in the Law He guides them away from the self-destructive customs of the nations. In the Gospel of Jesus Christ, believers have freedom from their sins, freedom to please God as His beloved, chosen people.

❖ **Lord, sustain us with the life-giving body and blood of Your Son. Amen.**

Remembrance of God's deliverance of the Israelites from Egypt was the most important component in their liturgical calendar. He made redemption the chief theme of their service. Jesus Christ, the Lamb of God, was slain on Good Friday as the Passover lambs were sacrificed. His sacrifice made redemption the chief theme of our worship too.

✤   **Blessed Redeemer, deliver us from all evil through Jesus Christ, our Paschal Lamb. Amen.**

By the Word of promise, the Lord grants us faith, that we may walk by faith and enjoy His blessings of abundance and peace. Failure to walk with God brings painful consequences (26:14–39). Therefore, cling to God's Word, especially His promise that His people belong to Him (26:13).

✦ **Lord, You alone have the words of eternal life. Amen.**

Just as the Lord consecrated the Levites to care for the tabernacle and to support the services of the sanctuary, He likewise calls and consecrates His people today to support the ministry of the Word. Rejoice in the mutual love and care He provides for all in Christ Jesus.

❖ **O God, bless our service together in spreading the Word of salvation to all nations. Amen.**

When you take a vow, honor the Lord by keeping your word. God, who does not take lightly any vow made to Him, faithfully keeps His vows, including that of Genesis 3:15, which promised your salvation in Christ.

❖ **Lord God, thank You for Your faithfulness. Help me to keep my word to You and to others. In Christ's name. Amen.**

No windows shed light into the Lord's sanctuary, so these lampstands are truly a light shining in the darkness, a poignant symbol that true light comes from the Lord alone. God's light is Jesus Christ (John 1:4), who conquers death and grants eternal life (Romans 6:23b).

❖ **Lord of heaven and earth, Your Word is a lamp to our feet and a light to our path. Amen.**

The Lord deals gently with His people by providing constant guidance and sound leadership. Today, pray for your leaders, that the Lord would bless and keep them and guide them in thoughtful service to His people, whom Christ redeemed with His precious blood.

✣ "Arise, O LORD, and let Your enemies be scattered, and let those who hate You flee before You" (10:35). Amen.

Like Moses, you may at times feel frustration and become angry with the Lord. Thanks be to God, He is "slow to anger and abounding in steadfast love and faithfulness" (Psalm 86:15).

✤   **Lord, You command us to call upon You in times of trouble, and You promise to deliver us. We thank You for hearing our prayer through Christ, our Lord. Amen.**

The land is just as God had described it to Moses, flowing with milk and honey. Yet 10 of the 12 spies fear the inhabitants of the land, thereby doubting God. When you face challenges, do not collapse in doubt. Instead, call on your gracious Lord, who redeemed you and will lead you.

✜   **Lord, forgive us for Christ's sake, and lead us through every trial. Amen.**

When the Lord's punishment falls on the rebels, the Lord's servant Aaron rushes into the midst of the plague to save the people. His intercession reminds us of Christ's intercession for us; He came among us to save us.

✤　**"Let my prayer be counted as incense before You, and the lifting up of my hands as the evening sacrifice!" (Psalm 141:2). Amen.**

When struggles and complaints hamper you, turn to the Lord in humble prayer. He will hear and honor your requests faithfully, in accordance with His good and gracious purposes.

✢ **Lord, we often doubt Your Word. Send Your Spirit to strengthen us, that we may pray confidently and lead boldly. Amen.**

As Moses guides God's people in the direction of the Red Sea, away from their primary objective of the Promised Land, rebellion begins anew. Our lives also persist in the pattern of rebellion, repentance, and restoration. Those who look upon the cross in faith are saved.

✤ **Gracious Lord, send Your Holy Spirit to deepen our faith in Christ, that we live by daily repentance and faith in Your Son. Amen.**

God allows no other gods before Him and takes necessary measures to preserve His people. He always gives Himself fully for His people as demonstrated by Christ's sacrifice on the cross for us.

❖   **Protect us, Lord, from the sin of idolatry. Grant us faithful ministers and leaders who will strengthen our faith by Your Word and Sacraments. Amen.**

Contrary to many grievances presented in Numbers, the daughters of Zelophehad approach Moses with humble demeanor to seek his counsel. The prayer of the upright pleases God (Proverbs 15:8). He has our good at heart in all His teaching.

❖ **Lord, grant us both boldness and humility in our prayers, that we may enjoy Your blessings and prosper before You. Amen.**

Consider how your choices will affect others. Pray for the Lord's guidance, and seek understanding in His Word. His Word to you is good, sealed in the promise of Christ Jesus, the head of His Bride, the Church.

❖ "Unless You build it, Father, The house is built in vain; Unless You, Savior, bless it, The joy will turn to pain. But nothing breaks the union Of hearts in You made one; The love Your Spirit hallows Is endless love begun." Amen. (*LSB* 858:4)

Vengeance belongs to God (Deuteronomy 32:35) and is enacted through His chosen authorities, not by individuals. Pray for the safety and peace of all in such callings. Entrust your life, health, and future to the one and only Savior, who is strong to deliver.

✜ "Entrust your days and burdens To God's most loving hand; He cares for you while ruling The sky, the sea, the land." Amen. (*LSB* 754:1)

The Lord calls us to fulfill our calling as His heaven-bound people. As you face new challenges, consider that the Lord has already prepared your way. His gift and inheritance cannot be taken from you.

❖   "Faint not nor fear, His arms are near; He changes not who holds you dear; Only believe, and you will see That Christ is all eternally." Amen. (*LSB* 664:4)

In Christ, God cares for each individual. He willingly bends an ear to hear even the most routine request and acts on each person's behalf with righteousness and mercy.

✢   Lord, You lovingly guided Your people Israel. You also found me in my sin and saved me through the precious blood of Your Son. Preserve me in the one true faith. Amen.

_____

_____

_____

_____

_____

_____

_____

_____

_____

_____

_____

_____

_____

_____

_____

_____

_____

_____

_____

_____

Through many trials, God raises a new generation in Israel and brings them to the plains of Moab just east of the Jordan River. God keeps His word to His people, including His word to you. Rejoice in the Lord's faithfulness as you share His testimonies with others. The Gospel is fresh and precious for every new generation.

✤   **Heavenly Lord, we praise You and thank You for Your faithfulness in Christ, our Lord. Amen.**

The Israelites' victories belong only to God. Our victories, too, belong to God. Our salvation is only by God's hand, not our own. By His Son's precious blood, we are justified; by His Spirit, we are sanctified.

✤   **Father, whenever we are tempted to boast of our own deeds, let us recall that "it is not the one who commends himself who is approved, but the one whom the Lord commends" (2 Corinthians 10:18). Amen.**

As He faithfully led Israel, God will also lead His people today. His promises to us are sealed in the blood of His Son (cf. 2 Corinthians 1:20).

✣   **Lord of heaven and earth, You shower Your blessings on those who are led to faith by Your Holy Spirit. Guide and protect us from the evil one, who would take away our promised inheritance. Amen.**

God lovingly establishes His ordinances, including the Ten Commandments. Through the Word, the Lord leads us to faith and to keep His commands faithfully; He shows forth His blessings in our lives.

✤ **Lord of all, we gratefully acknowledge that Christ has freed us from the bondage of the Law. Thanks be to God! Amen.**

Sinful men and women need an intermediary between themselves and God. Though Moses served in that capacity at Sinai, Jesus Christ fills that role in a much greater way for you and for me (1 Timothy 2:5–6; cf. Romans 8:1–2).

❖   **Through Christ, our Lord, draw us ever closer to You through Your Word and Sacraments. Amen.**

God desires to shower His people with blessings, but their hearing and following of His Word is required for Him to dwell among them. He alone is God. There is no other. Thankfully, the Father sent His one and only Son as our atoning sacrifice. God's Holy Spirit now dwells within all believers.

✤   **Lord, use us now as instruments for the salvation of others. Amen.**

_____

_____

_____

_____

_____

_____

_____

_____

_____

_____

_____

_____

_____

_____

_____

_____

_____

_____

_____

_____

_____

Today, through Jesus Christ, believers are led into the promised land of eternal life. Each time we look upon the empty cross, we are reminded of God's promise of redemption fulfilled in Christ.

✣　**Lord of all creation, we thank You for the precious foretelling of deliverance made known to Your ancient people and delivered in Christ Jesus, our Lord. Grant us encouragement in Your precious Word. Amen.**

How easily Christians today look upon themselves as self-made, dishonoring God in the process. Instead, may we pray as J. S. Bach did, "To God alone be glory" (*Soli Deo Gloria*), for there is no other Savior.

✠   **Father, forgive us. We ask that You send Your Holy Spirit to lead us to repentance, and then feed us with Your sustaining bread of life. Amen.**

God desires that all should be saved and learn of His coming Messiah, Jesus. By God's grace, we repent of our stubbornness. Through Baptism, we are made new creatures (Romans 6:4), counting ourselves dead to sin and alive to God (Romans 6:11).

✤ **Precious Lord, almighty Father, forgive us for the sake of Your dear Son. Amen.**

Although we have the Bible and know its teaching, we may fail to heed it. Pause today to repent and give praise to your Lord for His merciful goodness. Abundant blessings, especially eternal life (John 6:47), are still yours through Jesus Christ.

✣   **Lord and sustainer of life, make us new creatures who daily see Your abundant blessings and honor You with our lives. Amen.**

Those who oppose God can draw many followers through their displays of power and spectacle. God's Word gives us His solemn and binding promises. God means what He says: In Christ, your sins are forgiven. In Christ, you will find life to the full.

✤ **Father, by the leading of Your Holy Spirit, let me always trust in Your Son, my Lord Jesus Christ. Only in Him can I find the light, the truth, and the peace that I need. Amen.**

You can always be confident God will provide for you when you are in need, and that you can help others knowing that God will give you more than enough to live life to the full.

✛ **Gracious Father, since You have adopted me in Holy Baptism, help me give and receive in ways that honor You. Amen.**

DATE

TOPICS

Deuteronomy 16:1–17:20

God forbids all forms of false worship even as He provides for instruction in the truth. We did not choose God, but He chose us (John 15:16). We can be rightly confident that He will keep us in true faith and lead us through death to eternal life.

❖ **Lord Jesus, keep me in true faith so I may do those things that are pleasing to You. Amen.**

95

God has given us our own "city of refuge" to which we may flee when the guilt of sin threatens to overwhelm us: His grace in Christ Jesus, whose innocent blood was shed for sinners. There you will find free and full forgiveness—the guilt is purged away!

✛ **Almighty God, give to us a respect for all life as a sacred gift from You. Amen.**

In the face of danger, God encourages His people with the promise of His presence and the assurance that He fights for them to give them the victory. We, too, have been given the promise of our Savior's constant presence with us, even on the battlefields we tread.

✢   **Lord Jesus Christ, clothe us with the whole armor of God that we may stand firm in every assault and never lose sight of Your victory on our behalf at the cross and empty tomb. Amen.**

Since God is always with us, we dare not live as though He is not present or in ways that would dishonor Him. In Christ, we are assured that His love, forgiveness, and grace are always present and that He stands with us in our daily life as our sure defense.

✤ **O Lord God, thanks and praise to You that, as the new Israel, we are Your people, whom You save, sanctify, and grant ultimate victory. Amen.**

_____

_____

_____

_____

_____

_____

_____

_____

_____

_____

_____

_____

_____

_____

_____

_____

_____

_____

_____

_____

When we examine our words and actions, we must confess our failure to love our neighbor as we love ourselves. Thanks be to God for His compassion toward us! His Son loved us more than Himself, and He died for our sins.

❖ **Precious Savior, move me to love others more and more because of Your great love for me. Amen.**

People in every society sin by taking unfair advantage of one another. Such behavior stirs the Lord to anger. Only because Jesus bore our punishment can we escape God's wrath and receive full pardon for our sins.

✣   **Lord Jesus, may Your goodness lead me to be an instrument of justice and fairness in the world. Amen.**

_____

_____

_____

_____

_____

_____

_____

_____

_____

_____

_____

_____

_____

_____

_____

_____

_____

_____

_____

_____

_____

Israel broke the old covenant with their sins, as does everyone (cf. Jeremiah 31:31–34). But Jesus Christ is the mediator of a new covenant. His death redeems us "from the transgressions committed under the first covenant" (Hebrews 9:15).

✛   **Holy Spirit, comfort me with the sure knowledge that Christ has removed sin's curse. Amen.**

Threat and promise, Law and Gospel, are the ways of God with human-kind. Here, the blessings seal the renewal of the covenant, and the curses that follow anticipate the need for the new covenant, sealed in the blood of Christ, which was shed for our blessing and pardon.

❖ **Heavenly Father, give me a thankful heart and a desire to serve You and my neighbor. Amen.**

God has revealed what each one of us needs to know for eternal salvation, from our helplessness because of our sins to the sending of His Son to suffer and die to save us from these.

✤ **Lord, thank You for revealing to me the way of salvation. Grant me a bold heart to share this blessed truth with others. Amen.**

Moses taught the people, and teaches us, that a relationship with God means a circumcision of the heart, i.e., faith rooted in the heart and soul. Such faith lives in obedience to the one true God, who gathers and blesses His people.

✦ **Holy Spirit, circumcise our hearts through the Word so we cling to Christ in faith and walk in obedience to the Father. Amen.**

God in His mercy would go before His covenant people, destroy their enemies, and cause them to inherit the Promised Land. Because of the covenant of grace God made with His people, He would not leave them or forsake them.

❖   **Heavenly Father, when I feel alone and afraid, remind me that You will never leave me or forsake me. Amen.**

Employing enemy forces and the elements of nature, God would bring His calamity upon the Israelites. Yet, for His name's sake and in His compassion, He would vindicate His people and vanquish the enemy.

❖ **Father, through Your Spirit and Word, take away my heart of stone and create in me a new heart. In Jesus' name I pray. Amen.**

_____

_____

_____

_____

_____

_____

_____

_____

_____

_____

_____

_____

_____

_____

_____

_____

_____

_____

_____

_____

_____

The Messiah, unlike Moses, kept faith (cf. 32:51) and lived in perfect obedience to the Father. He secured the eternal promised land to prepare a place for all (John 14).

✤ **Father, bless me and make me a blessing to others so that I proclaim Your Word of salvation through Christ in this broken world. Amen.**

DATE

TOPICS

Although Moses disqualified himself from entering the Promised Land because of his disobedience, God allowed him to see firsthand the fulfillment of all Scripture, for Moses and us, at Christ's transfiguration.

✣   **Father, when I close my eyes in death, awaken me to behold Your glory and see You face-to-face, through Your Son, Jesus Christ. Amen.**

_____

_____

_____

_____

_____

_____

_____

_____

_____

_____

_____

_____

_____

_____

_____

_____

_____

_____

_____

_____

If left alone in our sin and weakness, we would not be able to serve God and to become successful in His eyes. Yet, God makes us strong and courageous for service by assuring us that through Immanuel ("God with us") we are forgiven and will inherit our eternal home (Hebrews 11:16).

❖　**Fill us, O Lord, with the promises of Your Word, that we may serve You with strength and courage and find success through You. Amen.**

DATE

TOPICS

Joshua 2:1–3:17

Our deepest human fears arise from a sense of guilt and the deserved judgment of God. But the God of free and faithful grace grants forgiveness, safety, and peace to repentant sinners, who are justified by grace through faith in Christ and who perform works that prove their God-given faith (Romans 3:22, 24; James 2:25–26).

✤ **We praise You, Lord, that You call people out of the darkness of their sin and into the light of Your grace. Amen.**

110

We sometimes ignore spiritual priorities while fretting over inferior matters. Awareness of God's saving grace and generous gifts leads us to set right priorities and to "seek first the kingdom of God and His righteousness" (Matthew 6:33).

✣ **Forgive our materialism, O Lord, and lead us to give priority to Your heavenly treasures. Amen.**

God is a God of justice, who cannot let sin go unpunished. Yet, God is also a God of love, whose justice was satisfied when His Son took the punishment for the sin of the world. The Lord delivers us, through faith in Jesus, from the destruction awaiting this present evil age.

❖ **We praise You, O Jesus, that You gave Yourself for our sins to deliver us from the present evil age. Amen.**

How often do we judge things based on appearance and act without consulting the Lord and His Word? His Word is a lamp to our feet and a light to our path.

❖   **Lord, grant us the wisdom and guidance of Your Spirit, so we might seek Your counsel in all we do. Amen.**

When confronted by strife, do we try to handle it ourselves, or do we call on the Lord to save and help us? What a blessing to call boldly on the Lord Jesus Christ in our troubles and find in His baptismal covenant with us grace and mercy to help in time of need.

✤ **Deliver us, good Lord, according to Your promises, for we trust in Your good Word. Amen.**

The Lord has said, "Do not be afraid" (11:6). Fear should not affect our faithfulness to the will and direction of the Lord. Jesus, by His faithfulness and His own hand, gives us the promised land of the new heavens and new earth as our eternal inheritance.

✣   **Gracious Lord, grant us faith in Your faithfulness, and accomplish Your service in and through us. Amen.**

The assigning of land to Judah points to our end-times promised land through Christ, who came from the tribe of Judah. As Judah was assigned land before fully possessing it, so the Lord gives us eternal life even before we fully possess it in the resurrection.

✤   **Lord, grant me faith to receive the promises You have laid before me for the sake of Your Son. Amen.**

The tribes of Joseph move to lay claim to the promises of God by inheriting their land. But they forget His promises about acquiring His blessings. God's promises do not come up short. He promises to address our true needs in Christ.

✤   **Dear God, help me to see how all of Your promises fit together and how well You have already acted to secure my portion in Your Son, my Lord and Savior Jesus Christ. Amen.**

God's servant Joshua needed to remind, encourage, and direct the people settling the land of Canaan, lest they become negligent in following God's promises to their completion. Take heart! God will not let His promised blessings go unused or unclaimed.

❖   **When we have received abundantly from You, O Lord, help us realize the fullness of Your blessings. Amen.**

We are not to become attached to the things of this world as though they have lasting value. As we seek first His kingdom and His righteousness through Christ, He will grant us what we need for this life (Matthew 6:33).

✣ **Heavenly Father, release us from worries and undue attachment to earthly things, so we might find our true joy in You and the enduring city awaiting us through Christ. Amen.**

Believers still carry their old sinful natures; therefore, misunderstandings or false accusations sometimes flare up among them. But the power of God's Word and Spirit working in our hearts can bring about genuine reconciliation and peace.

✤   O Lord, may Your name be blessed as Your Spirit cleans our ears of unfounded skepticism and our tongues of loveless criticism. Amen.

_____

What God threatens to those who reject Him and His salvation will certainly come to pass. God has not failed to fulfill even one word of all the good things He has promised. We can trust all the promises of His Word.

✤ **Lord, cause us to know that You are always faithful to Your Word, so that we heed Your warnings and trust Your gracious promises. Amen.**

We deserve none of the good that God gives us. God Himself in Christ has defeated our great enemies: sin, Satan, and death. He calls us by the Gospel of Christ and gives us an everlasting heritage, kingdom, and life.

✤ **Dear Lord of grace, make me know through Your Word that real success is not by my effort but by Your cross. Amen.**

_____

_____

_____

_____

_____

_____

_____

_____

_____

_____

_____

_____

_____

_____

_____

_____

_____

_____

_____

Jesus knows our weaknesses and forgives our neglect of His promises. Daily, we return to our Baptism to drown our sinful nature with its evil desires and to put on our new nature, which is righteous and pure. The righteousness of Jesus replaces our unrighteousness.

✤   **Thank You, Lord, for rescuing us from our own worst enemies—our sinful flesh and the "Canaanites" that surround us. Amen.**

Because of spiritual weakness, believers today also experience suffering, disappointments, and even death. Yet the Lord faithfully calls us to repentance amid our sufferings. He suffered for our sins and renews us by the Gospel.

❖ O Lord, "make us glad for as many days as You have afflicted us, and for as many years as we have seen evil" (Psalm 90:15). Amen.

_____

_____

_____

_____

_____

_____

_____

_____

_____

_____

_____

_____

_____

_____

_____

_____

_____

_____

_____

_____

Today, our struggles with temptation and problems may at times seem greater than we are able to bear. We may feel overwhelmed, confused, hopeless. Yet God's grace is sufficient for us, and His power is made perfect in weakness (2 Corinthians 12:9). In times of struggle, God's blessings may become most apparent and most treasured.

✤   **Assure us, O Lord, that Your grace is sufficient for all our needs. Grant us Your Spirit and boldness. Amen.**

We can be weak and slow to act. Yet the Lord is with us, alongside us. Jesus went ahead of us to the cross and through death to everlasting life. He will lead us to the victory ground of heaven.

❖ **Lord Jesus, give us faith to believe Your promises and courage to wage our battles and win the victory You give. Amen.**

In the same way the Lord fought for Gideon, so He also fights for us against seemingly insurmountable odds. He overcame our greatest enemy in the most improbable way: the sacrifice of Jesus on the cross.

✤   **Almighty God, Lord of hosts, encourage us with the assurance that You are with us always and that with You at our side, we never need fear. Amen.**

How blind we may be to the besetting sins of our culture! God's grace stepped into our world in the person of Jesus, who rode a donkey in humility so that He might teach and serve the people.

❖ **We praise You, O Lord, for the many blessings we enjoy through men and women who remain little known to us. We rejoice in the way Your Word focuses on the One we need to know most: Jesus. Amen.**

Christians may appear an unimportant minority on earth, with no particular claim to power, and losing influence as society becomes more and more secular. Yet God still guides the affairs of the world in the interest of His people.

❖ **Lord God, encourage us when we seem to be surrounded and overwhelmed by an ungodly world. Amen.**

Often, like Samson, it is when we are weak and broken spiritually (or perhaps also physically) that we finally despair of ourselves. In that hour, Christ is the true strong man for us spiritually. Samson carried the gates of a city, but Jesus carried the cross and all our sin.

❖ **O Lord, help me to trust not in my own strength but in the strength of Jesus Christ, my Lord, in whose name I pray. Amen.**

God's commands are often difficult to obey, but acting on our own impulses only multiplies sin. The Lord had generously provided the Danites with a sanctuary at Shiloh, where He promised to meet with them. The Lord meets with us and blesses us through the means He has ordained: the Word and the Sacraments.

✤   **O Lord, forgive my self-chosen theologies, my selfish cruelty to others, and my lack of trust. Amen.**

The violent death of a Levite's concubine illustrates the low point of wickedness during this period in Israel's history. Consider that such horrors happen still today and are even promoted under the guise of sexual or artistic freedom.

✠　O Lord, have pity! Deliver the Church, Your Bride, from evil. **Amen.**

These manipulations of morality are a final example of the moral degradation that comes from everyone doing what is right in his own eyes. God pours out His wrath on sinners, but He saves a remnant by His grace.

❖ O Lord, Your Word reveals the depths of my sin, including my misguided attempts at righteousness. Forgive me by the Word of Jesus, who gave His life to rescue me from sin. Amen.

You may struggle against unexpected changes in the economy or in your family. God gives you freedom in making family and business decisions, but He also gives you the blessings and guidance of His Holy Word. Look to the Word, wherein lies wisdom for this life and the promise of eternal life through Jesus.

✣   **Make my heart, Lord Jesus, captive to Your Word, which guides my family, my work, and my future. Amen.**

As the Lord blesses you, let others know of His kindness so that they may celebrate with you. He restores your life and guarantees your future through the blessings of His beloved Son.

✤ **Bless me, O Lord, that I may not fail to bless Your name before others and lead them in celebration of Your bountiful goodness. Amen.**

Everything that we have is a gift from the Lord. This means that we have no right to keep anything back from service to God, no matter how dear it is to us. Always true to His Word, He will stand by His promises to us, even when we have no earthly reason for hope.

❖   **Thank You, Lord, for all Your gifts to us. Let our joy be complete as we offer ourselves and our children to You and to each other in love. Amen.**

_____

_____

_____

_____

_____

_____

_____

_____

_____

_____

_____

_____

_____

_____

_____

_____

_____

_____

_____

_____

_____

Hannah's prayer stands as a warning to us when we are tempted to trust in our own strength, beauty, wealth, or intelligence. Her prayer also gives us encouragement to look to God for every good thing that we need in life, confident that He will fulfill our deepest desires in eternity through His Anointed One, Jesus Christ.

✦ **Praise to You, O God, for You delight in exalting those who humble themselves before You. Amen.**

The judgment against Eli is threatening also to us when we fail to restrain those under our authority who do evil. But also hear the assurance that human weakness will not thwart God's will to bring the Good News of salvation to His creation!

✤ **Lord, give us humility to receive and speak Your Word without fear of those who oppose You. Amen.**

God's word of judgment is fearful and means death to all who have sinned. Our hope lies in His mercy alone, shown in Christ Jesus, our faithful High Priest, who bore God's wrath.

✢ **Lord, let not my heart grow fat with self-righteousness, sloth, or indifference. Exercise me in Your life-giving Word. Amen.**

Today, we should not assume that our status as God's children through Holy Baptism means that we have the freedom to behave in an irreverent manner toward what God has set aside for holy purposes (e.g., the Lord's Supper). Instead, God has set us free to live in humility, repentance, and faith.

✤ **Thank You, Lord God, for consecrating us as Your holy people and for sharing Your holiness with us. Amen.**

Like the people of Israel, when we live apart from God, we experience frustration and defeat. As God leads us to cry to Him for mercy, He restores us and makes us whole in Christ Jesus.

✣   **Lord God, be merciful to us, for we have sinned against You. Give us Your peace, we ask, in Jesus' name. Amen.**

Like the people of Israel, our actions often say to God, "Not Your will, but mine be done," as we insist on things that may not be good for us. God often gives us what we want, but even more graciously, He gives us what we need—forgiveness, life, and salvation.

✢   **Dear Jesus, strengthen me to join You in praying, "Not my will, but Yours be done." Amen.**

The Lord's use of life's circumstances is beyond our expectations. He shows us His plans for us (Jeremiah 29:11), which ultimately are fulfilled in Jesus Christ (2 Corinthians 1:17–20). The events of our lives are never accidental but always providential.

❖   Give me the confidence of faith to look beyond the petty concerns of my daily life, Lord. Amen.

When circumstances call for boldness and righteous anger, do you act confidently? The Lord is our "very present help in trouble" (Psalm 46:1). In challenging times, God's Spirit empowers you to face the challenge.

❖   **O Holy Spirit, when I am to be an instrument of Your help or hope, give me Your words and gifts. In Jesus' name. Amen.**

When you look back over your life, see that you have been less than wholly faithful to the Lord. Yet, "consider what great things He has done for you" (v. 24). God remains faithful to His promises, especially His promise of forgiveness!

✠   **Lord, gracious Father, thank You for the blessings I have received from You, particularly the forgiveness of sins. Amen.**

True refuge resides only in the true God—the God of Abraham, Isaac, and Jacob, the God of Samuel, the God who fulfilled His promises by sending His Son, Jesus Christ, to save the world.

❖   Heavenly Father, we thank You for Your gracious daily guidance and protection. We ask that You continue to watch over us and those we love. You graciously give us all things through Your Son. Amen.

Too often, fear keeps us from venturing out for the Lord. Though we should not dare God to give us signs, we can learn from Jonathan's story to attempt great things for God and expect great things from Him. Though we may fail from the world's perspective, God gives us ultimate spiritual victory and all things in Christ.

❖ **Heavenly Father, inspire us through Jonathan's example to confront the forces of sin and Satan. Amen.**

God's Law is clear and calls for His people's perfect obedience in thought, word, and deed. Through the Law, God calls us to repent. Only because of Christ's sinless obedience and sacrificial death on our behalf can we enjoy His blessings.

✣ **Heavenly Father, forgive us for the many times we have not followed Your Word completely. Renew in us daily the will and ability to live for Him who died for us. Amen.**

Because God looks on our hearts (v. 7), we stand condemned before Him (Jeremiah 17:9–10a). By faith in the Gospel, our hearts are cleansed (Acts 15:9), and we are reassured that God will not despise a broken and contrite heart (Psalm 51:17).

❖ **Thank You, Lord, that You do not judge by appearances but have promised us that there is "no condemnation for those who are in Christ Jesus" (Romans 8:1). Amen.**

We are not to place our trust in human endeavors and devices. The message of the cross is that God chose what is weak to shame the strong, and the "weakness" of God is stronger than human strength (1 Corinthians 1:18–27; 1 John 4:4).

❖ **Lord God, when I feel insecure, let me cast my cares on You, knowing that You care for me. Amen.**

Saul's jealousy does him no good; meanwhile, David is faithful to the Lord, who gives him success. Envy and jealousy diminish our enjoyment of life, stealing our contentment. God "has blessed us in Christ with every spiritual blessing in the heavenly places" (Ephesians 1:3). What more do we need?

✜   **Lord, help me to be content with all the blessings You give me. Amen.**

When troubles and sins surround you, turn to the Lord and His servants for aid. Confess your sins and weaknesses honestly, and receive the care He administers through His servants. In mercy, the Lord will nourish, sustain, and forgive you.

✜ **Continue to nourish Your people and arm them against evil, dear Lord. Grant them wisdom with honesty. Amen.**

David had panicked due to fear (ch. 21), but the Lord calmed and directed him. When troubled, treasure God's Word as your stronghold. Through the Word, the Lord will bless, comfort, and strengthen you.

✤ **Give us a trusting heart to obey You, heavenly Father, and to live in the confidence of Your Word, our stronghold. Amen.**

The Lord reveals His will not only in the word of the prophet but also by hindsight in the unfolding of events. Trust the Lord to answer your prayers and to protect you against those who make themselves God's enemies. He is watching over you, though His presence may often be hidden by adverse circumstances.

✣   **Reveal to us Your will, dear Lord, and give us grace to follow it. Amen.**

David's compassion for vulnerable Saul is motivated by respect for God and His anointed. It is met warmly by Saul, resulting in a temporary truce. Today, be ready to show compassion even to your enemies, as God in Christ has demonstrated His undeserved love to you.

✤   **Gracious Lord, thank You for sending Your true Anointed One to bring mercy to me while I was Your enemy. Amen.**

DATE

TOPICS

1 Samuel 25:1–44

Angry decisions lead to self-destruction. God calls us to listen to the voice of reason and peace. His wisdom and peace, expressed in the godly counsel of His servants, will guide your heart in the way of life.

✤   **Father, give us grace to be like a prudent one who acts with knowledge, and not like a fool who flaunts his folly (Proverbs 13:16). Amen.**

Saul again pursues David, who demonstrates that he is a faithful, forgiving servant. Jesus, the Son of David, directs us to forgive "seventy times seven" (Matthew 18:22; without limit). He teaches this also by example, demonstrating His limitless forgiveness toward us.

✢ **Dearest Jesus, forgive us our trespasses, as we forgive those who trespass against us. Amen.**

When a spiritual vacuum exists, lost souls are drawn to the occult, despite warnings. Yet no genuine assurance will be found there. Acknowledge and rejoice that God's grace and promise are as close at hand as His Word, which will guide you in the paths of life.

❖   **Lord, when we are uncertain, grant us patience and comfort through Your Holy Word and the consolation of true brothers and sisters in the faith. Amen.**

The Lord aids David and the people of Ziklag through an unlikely source: an abandoned Egyptian slave. The Lord still provides for us through unlikely means, preeminently through Jesus' cross, by which He rescues us from Satan's hordes.

❖ **Deliver us from evil, O Lord, and strengthen us to assist others in their hour of crisis. Amen.**

There is no greater tragedy than when God's people compromise His Word, no greater blessing than when they steadfastly receive it. Learn by the examples of Saul and David. By promises and blessings, the King of heaven provides life for you in His Son, Jesus.

✣ **"Lord, keep us steadfast in Your Word; Curb those who by deceit or sword Would wrest the kingdom from Your Son And bring to naught all He has done." Amen.** (*LSB* **655:1**)

David may want to reign over all Israel right away, but that is not to be. Sometimes, God's promises call for patience. We have inherited the full kingdom of heaven through the innocent sufferings and death of Jesus, our Savior. We wait patiently to possess it.

❖ **Heavenly Father, give me patience as You fulfill Your promises in Your time. Amen.**

How easy for us to use dishonest methods as we strive for position and power. Self-interest and self-glory are sins that plague us all. Jesus, on the other hand, selflessly left His throne on high, died to pay for our sins on the cross, rose, and took the Church as His Bride.

✜ **Lord Jesus, praise be to Your holy name for Your supreme sacrifice on our behalf. Amen.**

David makes Jerusalem his capital over all Israel. The Lord causes this for the sake of His people. When success comes our way, let us not boast and demand recognition. Jesus, the Son of David, humbled Himself unto death, even death on a cross, for the sake of sinful people like us.

✤ **Lord, make me humble and give me Your blessings in Christ Jesus. Amen.**

In faithfully serving the Lord, are you willing to look foolish in the eyes of others? Do not fear to make merry before the Lord and endure suffering. Our Lord Jesus was not ashamed to humble Himself on the cross to save us from our arrogance.

❖ **Work true faithfulness in my life, O Lord, no matter how inappropriate it may be in the eyes of the world. Amen.**

_____

_____

_____

_____

_____

_____

_____

_____

_____

_____

_____

_____

_____

_____

_____

_____

_____

_____

_____

_____

In humility, David acknowledges that everything the Lord has done and will do for him and for Israel is due solely to the Lord's mercy. Today, when great blessing comes your way, glorify the Lord for His gifts. His greatest gift is the great One to come, Jesus, the Son of David.

✢   O Lord Jesus, make us truly thankful for Your mercy, and bless Your Church forever. Amen.

We are in a battle against temptation and sin. As it was for David, our victory comes only when the Lord gives it. Beginning in Baptism and through faith in Jesus Christ, the Lord gives us Christ's blood-bought victory over sin, death, and the devil.

✤ **Gracious Lord, forgive my sins and keep my faith in the one glorious victory won by Jesus Christ. Amen.**

Whenever you try to hide a sin by committing another sin, you are just digging yourself deeper into a hole. Instead, confess! God will forgive all who repent and seek the forgiveness earned by Christ on the cross.

✣ **"Lord Jesus, think on me And purge away my sin; From worldly passions set me free And make me pure within."** Amen. (*LSB* **610:1**)

While our sin does not always lead to outright murder, unrepentant sin does lead to our spiritual death and to much grief. True reconciliation with God is granted us through the forgiveness of our sins, through the atoning death of God's own Son.

✠ **O Lord Jesus, Son of David, have mercy on us! Pardon our iniquity, and with Your forgiveness bring an end to the warfare of our sin. Amen.**

_____

_____

_____

_____

_____

_____

_____

_____

_____

_____

_____

_____

_____

_____

_____

_____

_____

_____

_____

_____

_____

_____

Life here in this world is often a wilderness journey of weeping and the expectation of death. This is due to our sin against God. But Christ has gone the way of sorrows on our behalf, that we might cross the Jordan with Him, through the waters of Holy Baptism, out of the wilderness into the promised land of heaven.

✣ **O Lord Jesus Christ, by the blood of Your eternal covenant, preserve our faith and bring us at last into Your kingdom. Amen.**

Official messengers must be faithful in delivering the news given them to tell, even if their message is not welcome. This holds true especially for ministers of the Gospel. How blessed are the feet of those who proclaim the Gospel, who tell us that our King Jesus reigns with mercy!

❖   **Heavenly Father, give us courage to speak Your Word according to our vocation as Christians. Amen.**

_____

_____

_____

_____

_____

_____

_____

_____

_____

_____

_____

_____

_____

_____

_____

_____

_____

_____

_____

_____

Sometimes our sin is manifested in pride and self-righteousness, other times in despondency and defeatism. Like Joab, the Law confronts us with what we must do. But God our King speaks kindly to us. He did not spare His own Son but gave Him up for us all.

✤   **Dear Father in heaven, give us the victory by the death and resurrection of Your only-begotten Son. Amen.**

David acknowledges that God Almighty trained him for war, provided him with weapons of war, fought for him, and gained for him the victory. Whatever good is in us is God's gift alone. Likewise, forgiveness of our sins and victory over our spiritual enemies are purely His gifts.

✤   **Father, Son, and Holy Spirit, with David I praise You for delivering me from the power of evil. Amen.**

David speaks forth his last will and testament, prophesying of God's eternal covenant, which would be fulfilled in the kingdom of Christ. In the Scriptures, God sets forth His covenant of grace, an eternal covenant in which Christ rules us, justifies us, and brings us to eternal life.

✢   **O God of Israel, rule us, save us, and bring us into Your heavenly kingdom. Amen.**

Pestilence led to David's repentance, repentance led to sacrifice, and sacrifice led to the temple—the place of God's mercy on earth. Likewise, Christ's cross was a sacrifice to appease God's wrath, which now has resulted in the place of God's mercy on earth: the means of grace in the Holy Christian Church.

✢   "All sins Thou borest for us, Else had despair reigned o'er us: Have mercy on us, O Jesus!" Amen. (LSB 434:1)

DATE

TOPICS

David's dying example of concern for his son Solomon, and the kingdom over which he would reign, encourages us in Christlike love and service to our families and others. In His death, Christ supplied fully for our life and peaceable service in His kingdom.

✣ **Father in heaven, through life and in the hour of death, keep my eyes set on my Lord and Savior Jesus Christ. Amen.**

True wisdom consists of far more than acquiring facts and information. Rather, it is godly wisdom to declare our sinfulness and need for a Savior, and to see in Jesus the One who meets all our needs.

✤ Omniscient Lord, wisdom's highest treasure resides in Your Son, who is the very Wisdom of God. Guide me constantly to serve You faithfully. Amen.

_____

_____

_____

_____

_____

_____

_____

_____

_____

_____

_____

_____

_____

_____

_____

_____

_____

_____

_____

_____

_____

_____

With what care and dedication Solomon builds! The Lord calls us to show equal concern for the house of worship in which we gather. It is, after all, a reflection of our devotion to the Lord, His Word, and His work. His dedication to us appeared in Solomon's descendant Jesus, whose body as a holy temple secured our salvation.

❖ **Lord of hosts, forgive our sins, and enable us to serve You and work with our neighbors. Through Jesus' name. Amen.**

The thousands of sacrifices at the temple prefigure the one sacrifice when Jesus Christ, the great High Priest, offered His life for the sins of the world. We offer our lives as living sacrifices for our Lord and Savior, having received the priceless gift of salvation through Him.

✢ **Loving Savior, thousand, thousand thanks are Yours for the great sacrifice You made on the cross for the sins of the world. Amen.**

We often complain about not having enough of this world's goods, yet God daily and richly forgives us and continues to shower material blessings upon us. How great is His undeserved goodness! Such is His great love toward us in Christ—becoming poor, that we might be rich.

✜ **Almighty Lord, Ruler of earth and sea, all things on earth are Yours. We praise You for Your all-surpassing greatness. Amen.**

We dare never take God's grace lightly, thinking we can sin without consequences. May God the Holy Spirit always keep us focused on our Savior through Word and Sacraments. Jesus did not take us for granted; He saved us with precious grace.

✜   **Blest Savior dear, be always near. Keep me from evil, harm, and fear. Amen.**

Today, we need to be aware of the subtle giving of our hearts to the idols of false religions, materialism, pleasure, and self-centeredness. The Lord turns us away from these traps and leads us to the worship of the true God, our Savior, who created the heavens and the earth.

✣ **Lord, give us godly wisdom to avoid the errors of the past and follow what is good and right. In Jesus' name. Amen.**

Sin and rebellion against God are not limited by politics or geography. No one is immune from God's judgment. Pray that God in His mercy will forgive and spare the new Israel, the Church, for the sake of Jesus, the Savior. His faithful reign extends to all people.

❖ **Lord God Almighty, send Your Holy Spirit to enlighten and strengthen us, that we may not fall into sin and unbelief. In the Savior's name we pray. Amen.**

Once people reject God's Word, anything goes, as the lives of Ahab and Jezebel attest. Yet by His grace, God can call people from the deepest shadow of darkness to repentance and salvation. In Christ, we have the light of life; in Him, we receive the grace and love of our heavenly Father.

✥ **"Renew me, O eternal Light, And let my heart and soul be bright, Illumined with the light of grace That issues from Your holy face." Amen.** (*LSB* 704:1)

God makes sure that truth ultimately prevails. No matter how entrenched and powerful the forces of evil are in the world, God is still guiding history for the good of His people, for their everlasting salvation.

❖ **Lord God, how bold the wicked are, yet I know that You will always be with those whom You have brought into Your family by faith in Jesus Christ. Amen.**

God's voice speaks to us in the quietness of the inspired pages of Scripture, by which He encourages us with the forgiveness, life, and salvation in Jesus, the Word made flesh.

✣ **I thank You, dear God, that in the pages of the Bible, You have come with the assuring whisper of Your presence and protection. In the gentle Savior's name. Amen.**

The Lord guides history and even uses evil people for His good purposes. In such records, the Lord teaches us how He punishes the godless and protects those who call on His name. While the Bible records battles and wars, behind it all, God is still in control for the sake of His people.

❖ **Lord of the nations, amid the upheavals and wars of this sinful world, guide, strengthen, encourage, and uplift Your people. Amen.**

_____

_____

_____

_____

_____

_____

_____

_____

_____

_____

_____

_____

_____

_____

_____

_____

_____

_____

_____

_____

_____

We are constantly tempted to get what we want at the expense of others. Instead of taking from others, Jesus gave Himself for us. In sacrificing His life for the sins of the world, He gave us the priceless treasure of life and salvation.

✤ **Lord Jesus, touch our cold and loveless hearts, and fill them with the warmth of Your love, that we may reach out to all who are in need. Amen.**

As the Lord calls you to service, He will prepare and support you. Though miracles may not follow you (as with Elisha), you have God's miraculous Word in the pages of Holy Scripture by which the Lord will bless you with the comfort of salvation and equip you for every good work.

✣   **O Lord, as You bore insult on the cross and brought forth life for me, let me bear all insults and burdens of my calling. Amen.**

_____

_____

_____

_____

_____

_____

_____

_____

_____

_____

_____

_____

_____

_____

_____

_____

_____

_____

The Shunammite woman passionately seeks the Lord's help for her son by seeking out Elisha. When you seek the Lord in prayer, pour out your heart to Him. Bow before Him and make your petitions known. The Lord has made His heart known for you in the life, death, and resurrection of His only-begotten Son, our Savior.

❖   **Hear me, O Lord, when I cry to You. Answer me according to Your mercy. Amen.**

_____

_____

_____

_____

_____

_____

_____

_____

_____

_____

_____

_____

_____

_____

_____

_____

_____

_____

When you are caught in sin, do not hesitate to acknowledge your deeds before the Lord. He is rich in mercy toward the brokenhearted and all who confess their needs to Him.

✦ **Lord, grant me a steadfast heart and sincere repentance, that I may inherit the wealth of Your grace in Christ. Amen.**

_____

_____

_____

_____

_____

_____

_____

_____

_____

_____

_____

_____

_____

_____

_____

_____

_____

_____

_____

_____

_____

God's promises always seem too good to be true. Yet He provided bread from heaven to Israel in the wilderness (Exodus 16:4–31) and today sustains us with the true bread of heaven, the life-giving body of Jesus in the Sacrament of the Altar.

✠ **Sustain me, O Lord, against the devil's siege, my doubts, and the world's temptations. Amen.**

Today, when temptation confronts you, do not test the Lord's patience by making peace with wickedness or ungodly relationships but pray that He would guide you through the Word into wholesome relationships. His Word is a lamp for your feet and enlightenment for life everlasting in Christ.

✛ **Enlighten us, Lord, by the light of Your Christ, and preserve Your people. Amen.**

_____

_____

_____

_____

_____

_____

_____

_____

_____

_____

_____

_____

_____

_____

_____

_____

_____

_____

_____

_____

Despite Jehu's unwillingness to follow the Lord's Word completely, the Lord brought the prophecy to absolute completion through trampling horses and biting dogs. Not a letter of His Word shall fail! Though we fail, God's Word will and does succeed for His sake and for our sakes in Christ the Savior.

✣   **King of heaven, reign in justice and compassion for the sake of Your Church. Amen.**

_____

_____

_____

_____

_____

_____

_____

_____

_____

_____

_____

_____

_____

_____

_____

_____

_____

_____

_____

_____

_____

Joash, who began so well, comes to a sorrowful end because he departs from the Lord's way. Through faith, let the end of your life honor your Savior and your heritage. Jesus, who abides with you always, will day by day forgive your faults and deliver you from temptation. His instruction and presence are everlasting.

✜ **O Lord, let Your mercies be new for me every morning to the end of my days. Amen.**

_____

_____

_____

_____

_____

_____

_____

_____

_____

_____

_____

_____

_____

_____

_____

_____

_____

_____

_____

_____

The Lord again shows remarkable patience for His rebellious people on the basis of His promises and compassion. If members of your family have wandered from the faith they professed before the Church, do not stop praying for them or proclaiming the Word to them. With the Lord there is great compassion, and His promises uphold us.

✢ **Lord, grant restoration to those who wander. Amen.**

When times are difficult, you may feel tempted to turn on those close to you, but that will only bring further despair. Instead, turn to the Lord in prayer, requesting peace and unity through the Gospel, which unites God's people through Baptism in His name and communion in His Supper.

✣   **Lord, move us to pray for one another and to support one another in peace. Amen.**

The Lord had commanded Israel to deal graciously with sojourners and to teach them the faith and practices of the true God. He would have us deal kindly and patiently with sojourners and guests among us, proclaiming to them God's Law and Gospel, by which the Lord consecrates for Himself a people.

❖ **Lord, grant me an open heart to share Your Word. Amen.**

Placing Sennacherib's words before the Lord, Hezekiah asks the Lord to distinguish Himself from the idols of the nations. When you pray, appeal to the Lord on the basis of His Word, which describes His unique attributes. The Lord will hear your prayer for Jesus' sake and will answer faithfully.

✢   **O Lord God, please save us, that all the kingdoms of the earth may know that You, O Lord, are God alone. Amen.**

_____

_____

_____

_____

_____

_____

_____

_____

_____

_____

_____

_____

_____

_____

_____

_____

_____

_____

_____

_____

_____

_____

Call on the Lord, as He invites you to do, and trust, like faithful Hezekiah, that the Lord indeed hears and answers for His mercy's sake, which He has revealed to us in Christ.

❖   **O Lord, remember me, and hear my daily requests for the sake of Your promises through Jesus. Amen.**

Today, rather than test God's patience, make daily repentance part of your life. For such repentance to be faithful and not just routine, cling to the teachings of God's Word, which shows you your sins and the ways of God's heritage. The Lord will prosper you in His way and regard you as His dear child.

✦ **Merciful Father, You are our shield and portion. Preserve Your heritage, we pray. Amen.**

Today, the Lord may call you to take bold action. Set your heart to serve the Lord and pray for His help to make changes peaceably. In all circumstances, the God of peace will sustain you for good works. Best of all, He has accomplished your salvation through His beloved Son.

❖ **Give me a soft heart toward You, O Lord, but a firm heart toward those who seek to overthrow Your ways. Amen.**

With God's counsel, adjust to the disappointments you face and make different plans for the future. Most of all, repent of your failures and confess your shortcomings. Your Lord yet has great blessings in mind for you, which He grants in Christ.

❖ **Turn my face, O Lord, in the way that I should go. Quiet my heart and grant me hope for the future. Amen.**

These genealogies show how the Lord continues to work through families as the faith is preserved and spread from one generation to the next. The Godhead itself shows this, with the Father sending forth His Son for the sake of our salvation (John 3:16).

✤   **Merciful Father, draw us together with cords of love through Your Son. Amen.**

Leadership and inheritance are not blessings one can simply take for granted, because they come with responsibility. God has given you responsibility in His kingdom, no matter what your standing in life. He has also equipped and blessed you with gifts, including the blessings of life and salvation through Christ, our Head.

✢   **Lead on, dearest Jesus, and grant me the will and strength to follow Your way. Amen.**

The separated people of Israel return to a new unity at Jerusalem. The Lord renews their service and their hope based on restored faith in His mercy. Though we break faith with the Lord daily, He restores us daily through repentance and faith in Christ, whose mercy is new every morning.

✠ **Renew us, Lord. Recall us to Zion, and sanctify our service by Your Word. Amen.**

David inquires of and relies on the Lord for victory. For our plans to have God's blessing, we must call on Him and submit to the judgment of His Word. Yet when we are weak, the Lord Himself will fight for us, especially against sin, death, and the devil.

✤ **Lord Jesus, be my King and burst through all enemies that would separate me from You. Amen.**

Three psalms are arranged specifically to emphasize Israel's thanks for the Lord's merciful deeds. Recite David's Song to express your thanks to God, including specific examples of His mercy in your life. For His steadfast love, which He professes to you through His beloved Son, truly endures forever.

❖   **"Blessed be the Lᴏʀᴅ, the God of Israel, from everlasting to everlasting!" (16:36). Amen.**

In all we do for the Lord, we must first consult His Word to find out what is pleasing to Him. Jesus Christ is the "rest" and "house" promised to David. In Him, God's people have rest from their enemies of sin and death, and in Him they shall dwell forever.

❖ **Gracious Lord, keep us in the true faith, that we may have the blessed rest and peace that Christ alone provides. Amen.**

_____

_____

_____

_____

_____

_____

_____

_____

_____

_____

_____

_____

_____

_____

_____

_____

_____

_____

_____

_____

Fear of such giants had kept Israel from entering the Promised Land, but the Lord strengthened His people for victory. No matter what colossal challenges face you, the Lord will grant you strength and faithful companions with whom to overcome such challenges.

❖ **Lord, equip me with all things needful to fulfill Your calling. Grant me the support of dear brothers and sisters who take confidence in Your promises, through Christ, our Lord. Amen.**

Pestilence led to David's repentance, repentance led to sacrifice, and sacrifice led to the temple—the place of God's mercy on earth. Likewise, Christ's cross was a sacrifice to appease God's wrath, which now has resulted in the place of God's mercy on earth: the means of grace in the Holy Christian Church.

❖ **"All sins Thou borest for us, Else had despair reigned o'er us: Have mercy on us, O Jesus!" Amen.** (*LSB* 434:1)

_____

_____

_____

_____

_____

_____

_____

_____

_____

_____

_____

_____

_____

_____

_____

_____

_____

_____

_____

_____

_____

_____

Our success and our future is with the Lord. He entrusted the work of our salvation to His beloved Son, who in turn commended the temple of His body and His spirit into the Father's hands (Luke 23:46), that we might be cleansed by His blood and reign with Him in the resurrection.

❖ **O Jesus, grant such trust and sharing in our families! Be with us, and keep us by Your grace. Amen.**

As the Lord granted David wisdom to pursue his calling, He will grant you wisdom for your calling. Like David, listen to the wisdom of your family and counselors, but consider all things in view of God's Word. Through the Word, the Lord saves you from sin and from foolish error in your service.

✥   **O Lord, grant me Your wisdom and counsel. Amen.**

God calls parents to hear Him through Holy Scripture and to pass these words and duties along to their heirs. How rich is our inheritance through the Word, which consecrates us as co-heirs with Christ and as the temple of the living God.

✤ **Hallowed Father, make me holy by the blood of Your Son, that I may inherit the riches of Your grace and the gift of Your Spirit. Amen.**

Everything you have comes from God's bountiful goodness; therefore, give generously to the work of His Church and set a good example for those under your care. The Lord gives Himself to you with a whole heart and would not withhold His only-begotten Son.

✜ **Bless me, O Lord, that I may bless and freely give all honor to Your saving name. Amen.**

As the Lord blesses your service, use your gifts to bless those who work with you and for you. Remember how the Lord works on your behalf in all things, and how He administers the greatest blessings of all: the treasures of His mercy in Christ.

✣ **O Lord, I yield my treasure, my life, and all things in wise service to Your kingdom and care for my neighbor. Amen.**

_____
_____
_____
_____
_____
_____
_____
_____
_____
_____
_____
_____
_____
_____
_____
_____
_____
_____
_____

Solomon's magnificent temple with its furnishings, especially those relating to the sacrificial system, point to the coming Savior. Through Jesus' blood and merit, all our sins are washed away. Through the Savior's long-promised sacrifice, forgiveness, life, and eternal salvation are ours. Thanks be to God!

✤ **Savior of the nations, dwell in my heart, and make it a temple set apart for loving service to You. Amen.**

_____

_____

_____

_____

_____

_____

_____

_____

_____

_____

_____

_____

_____

_____

_____

_____

_____

_____

_____

_____

_____

_____

_____

The Lord shows His approval of the temple by igniting the sacrifices and filling the temple with His glory. Many people crave such miracles and affirmation for their work and decisions. Remember that in all things the Lord guides us through His Word, which ignites our hearts and fills our minds with His affirmation.

✢ **Move my heart to trust You, Lord, whether or not I witness miracles. Ever lead me by Your affirming Word. Amen.**

Not only does God bless Solomon with great wisdom, but He also blesses him with a great reputation. May we humbly recognize that the blessings we enjoy—including earthly prosperity and a good name—come to us by God's undeserved grace in His Son, Jesus.

✤ **Everlasting King, teach me to lean not on my own understanding but on the wisdom that abounds in Your Holy Word. Amen.**

_____

_____

_____

_____

_____

_____

_____

_____

_____

_____

_____

_____

_____

_____

_____

_____

_____

_____

_____

_____

_____

When faithfulness to the Lord comes with challenges, still choose to follow the way of faithfulness, seeking the fellowship of the faithful in the Church. Your Lord, who is always faithful, will strengthen and sustain you in the fellowship of His Word and Sacraments.

✣   **Deliver us from evil, O Lord, and grant us faithful leaders and fellow believers who can help us in our time of need. Amen.**

The Lord proves Himself righteous toward Rehoboam and Judah by punishing their abandonment of His Law and by hearing their confession of sin. The Lord is always ready to hear our confession and to forgive us. In applying His Law, He always has in mind our good, our repentance, and our salvation.

✤   **Hear my cry, O righteous Lord, and answer me according to Your mercy in Christ. Amen.**

The Lord fights against Jeroboam for the sake of Abijah and Judah. Today, when trouble assails and surrounds you, call out confidently to the Lord. He fights mightily on your behalf and in ways beyond your comprehension, as demonstrated in His victory over Satan at the cross.

✤   **Hear my cry, O Mighty Ruler, and overthrow the enemies of Your kingdom. Amen.**

Asa stumbles in his faith, but rather than repent, he foolishly lashes out at the Lord's prophet. You, too, will stumble. In every challenge, daily rely on the Lord by calling on Him in prayer and by requesting His forgiveness. Because of His righteousness, He will declare you blameless for the sake of His Son.

✣ **O Lord, give me Your strong support, for I rely on You alone. Amen.**

_____

_____

_____

_____

_____

_____

_____

_____

_____

_____

_____

_____

_____

_____

_____

_____

_____

_____

_____

_____

The Lord strengthens faithful Jehoshaphat so that the fear of the Lord falls upon the nations. As the Lord strengthens you, use that strength to honor His name. He desires salvation and peace for all people, as taught in His Word.

❖ **Lord, provide us with strength in all realms of our lives, that we may in every way give testimony to Your generosity. Amen.**

The Lord calls Jehoshaphat to serve Him with His whole heart—halfhearted commitment simply will not do. This is no less true for us. The Lord desires our wholehearted commitment, for He committed Himself wholly to us in the person of His beloved Son.

❖ **Dearest Lord, I yield my whole heart to Your service, that reform may begin with me. Amen.**

Through a letter from Elijah the prophet, the Lord warns Jehoram that he must face God's punishment. A harsh letter is difficult to write and harder still to receive. Yet as sinners, we all need the rebuke of God's Law against our sins. Above all, we need the call to repentance, forgiveness, and new life that the Lord is always ready to offer.

✤ **Lord, lead me to receive Your Word as a letter for my instruction and restoration. Amen.**

Each of us needs good counsel, especially God's Law and Gospel, which reveal the Lord's ways to us. When others point out your weaknesses, do not harden your heart toward them or toward the Lord. The Lord's great desire is to bring you back, restoring you through confession and forgiveness.

✤ **Call me back to You, O Lord, through the faithful words of Your prophets. Amen.**

Though the Lord grants him victories, Amaziah continues in rebellion. Today, we likewise feel the constant pressure to compromise the truth and follow the Lord halfheartedly. By His faithful and gracious Word, the Lord, who has power to help, will unstop our ears and turn our hearts to hear Him.

❖ **Speak, O Lord, that I may know Your ways and walk in them by faith. Amen.**

Mistreating one's relatives, as the Israelites did, is doubly shameful. God calls us to treat our extended family with respect and care to lead them to repentance and life. Thankfully, the Lord treats us mercifully by forgiving our sins and reconciling us to the family of God.

✤   **Grant our families peace and unity, O Lord, that we may extend Your kindness to all. Amen.**

The bloody sacrifices at the temple cleanse God's repentant people from their sins, anticipating Christ's perfect sacrifice on the cross. Today, the Lord cleanses and consecrates us through Holy Baptism, for in Baptism we are joined to Christ's atoning death and resurrection.

✤ O Lord, consecrate Your servants, that we may offer sincere worship in Your name. Amen.

Hezekiah renews the Passover celebration to call the people back to the Lord. Today, we regularly celebrate the new Passover—the Holy Supper of Christ, who offered Himself in compassion for our salvation.

✦   **Grant that I return to You, blessed Lamb of God, and have one heart with my brothers and sisters. Amen.**

Even if you are able to fend off all other threats, pride will still assault and defeat you if the Lord does not come to your aid. Like Hezekiah, humble yourself before the Lord and ask for His forgiveness. Recognize your successes as signs of His kindness, which He extends through the blessings of creation and the mercy of Jesus Christ.

✛ **Grant me sincere humility, O Lord, like that of Jesus. Amen.**

Like a patient father, the Lord disciplines us and even allows us to learn our lessons the hard way, through error and pain. Yet He is always ready to hear us, just as He heard and had compassion on the wicked king Manasseh.

❖ **O Lord, instruct me through the words of Your prophets, and grant me sincere repentance day by day, that I may know You alone as my God. Amen.**

Sincere faith is expressed not only by service to the Lord but also by leaving behind and removing those things that tempt us and would divide our devotion. The Holy Spirit will lead you not only to confess your sin but also to put away and avoid temptation. The Lord alone is your God; He is the only Savior.

❖ **O one true God, grant me an undivided heart, that I may serve You truly. Amen.**

Always check your will against God's will, recorded in Scripture, so that He may teach you persistence in faith and break your sinful stubbornness. Thanks be to God, He has a remedy for all your faults through His gift of forgiveness, His Spirit, and instruction in righteousness.

❖ **Remedy my faults, Great Physician, and grant me a willing heart to believe Your Word. Amen.**

_____

_____

_____

_____

_____

_____

_____

_____

_____

_____

_____

_____

_____

_____

_____

_____

_____

_____

_____

The Lord of heaven and earth continues to govern the nations for the good of His people. Though the news we hear each day is often bad, we can rejoice that the Lord of heaven is at work amid tumultuous events. Consider how He wrought our salvation through the decisions of Roman and Judean rulers who crucified our Savior!

✤   **Lord of history, stir my heart to praise You and to serve my neighbor according to Your merciful goodness. Amen.**

Through Scripture, keep aware of spiritual struggles and make them the focus of your prayers against Satan. Take courage from the Lord's mastery of His creation and the manner in which He works for the good of His people, especially shown in the civil punishment and glorious resurrection of His Son for our redemption.

❖ **Hear the cry of Your people, mighty King, and work among us for our blessing. Amen.**

God's prophets boldly call His people back to the work of the Jerusalem temple. When your cause is right in the Lord's eyes, do not hesitate to act and to call others to peaceable action. Act confidently, because the Lord will watch over you, bless you, and keep you through Christ.

❖ **Stir Your people to bold action, O Lord, in the cause of pure and faithful worship. Amen.**

Through the decree of the pagan ruler Artaxerxes, the Lord provides for the instruction of His people in His Word, as led by Ezra. Though the emperor provides numerous gifts, God's Word stands out as the greatest gift, by which the Lord converts hearts and extends His gracious rule.

✢ **We bless You, O Lord, for Your good Word, delivered for our salvation. Amen.**

_____

_____

_____

_____

_____

_____

_____

_____

_____

_____

_____

_____

_____

_____

_____

_____

_____

_____

_____

_____

These events teach us about the gravity of God's Law, of marriage, and of vows. Enter into such matters thoughtfully and informed by God's Word. The Lord Himself has vowed to guide and care for your family and to save you through the life of His Son, Jesus.

❖   **Lord, lead me to understand and keep my vows and to bring honor to my family and to Your name. Amen.**

_____

_____

_____

_____

_____

_____

_____

_____

_____

_____

_____

_____

_____

_____

_____

_____

_____

_____

_____

_____

As you hear of other people's needs, take them to heart as a matter of prayer and concern. Your gracious Savior, who knows and bears all your cares, will likewise care for you as you support your brothers and sisters in Christ.

❖   **O Lord, hear my plea for those in need, and grant me a heart ready to serve them. Amen.**

As the Lord gives you strength, support the good works of others, which creates life and improves its quality. The Lord Jesus, who passed through the gates of Jerusalem, will sanctify your service through the blessings of His Word and in answer to your prayers.

❖ **Open to me, O Lord, the gates of heaven, that I may enter there by Your grace alone. Amen.**

Do not let the taunts of unbelievers or naysayers keep you from fulfilling your calling. The great and powerful Lord—He who stooped to bear our burdens and save us in Christ—is with you in your work.

✤ **Great and awesome Lord, I remember and praise Your good works. Work on my behalf, O Lord, that I may fulfill Your purpose for me. Amen.**

By studying Scripture, the Judeans learned that they had overlooked celebrating a key feast. How often we may overlook God's teachings because we do not know the Word! Consume and study the Scriptures daily, for by them the Lord nurtures faith and grants life.

✜   **I rejoice, O Savior, in the goodness of Your Word, my daily good news in this sad, sin-broken world. Amen.**

The people confess the Lord's enduring mercy promised in the covenant. They were saved by God's grace, not by their obedience. You, too, are saved only by God's grace, which He offers faithfully through Christ Jesus.

✤   **We confess You alone, O Lord, our Maker, Redeemer, and Sanctifier. Amen.**

As you serve the Lord, you will also have frustrating experiences. Pray for the Lord to grant you strength as a leader, to control your anger, and to maintain proper focus on the Word. When frustration gets the better of you, count on the Lord to forgive you and strengthen you for continued service.

✤   **Remember, O my God, the needs of Your people, and give us grace under pressure. Amen.**

God will often use evil deeds to work His will. Joseph said to his brothers, "You meant evil against me, but God meant it for good" (Genesis 50:20). Nothing demonstrates this truth more clearly than Jesus' death on the cross. Because of His death, we have life.

✢   **Heavenly King, help me remember that You rule over all things and can bring good from evil. Amen.**

_____

_____

_____

_____

_____

_____

_____

_____

_____

_____

_____

_____

_____

_____

_____

_____

_____

_____

_____

Like Esther, God may provide us with positions, wealth, and talents that enable us to serve the cause of God's people and the Gospel. Yet we all have been guilty of exhibiting weak faith by our failure to act. Thanks be to God that He sent our Deliverer to redeem us from every failure.

✢ **Dear Jesus, Your kingdom expands through Word and Sacraments. Grant me golden opportunities to be Your witness. Amen.**

It is God who inspires Esther's delay in order to give Haman more rope with which to hang himself. We are often impatient, eager to hurry things along. When God seems to act too slowly on our behalf, we may still trust His wisdom and continue to pray with confidence, "Your good and gracious will be done."

✠   **Loving Father, give me patience to wait in hope for Your saving help. Amen.**

God controls history to preserve His elect and fulfill His promises. That is still true today. The Church has been called to witness to the Gospel in a world that is often contemptuous and hostile. God keeps us close to our Savior so that we might be His throughout all eternity.

❖ **Praise be to Your name, Lord God, for calling me to faith in Your Son and promising Your loving protection for me and all believers, now and forever. Amen.**

Is the Lord sacrificing Job to His own pride? No! The Lord also puts Satan to the test in order to prove something marvelous for you: Satan cannot snatch you out of the Lord's hand (John 10:28–29).

❖ **Though suffering and doubt grip me, O Lord, You cling to me and will never forsake me. Amen.**

DATE

TOPICS

Job feels there is nothing he can do. Though he certainly cannot aid himself, he can pray for the Lord's deliverance. This is the Lord's promise and great comfort in the face of all adversity: We can call on the Lord Almighty in prayer; He has promised to answer.

✣ **Lord, lead us to call upon Your name in every trouble, pray, praise, and give thanks. Amen.**

When you reach out to a friend or family member, do not give answers that simply bandage deep hurts. Listen carefully to and learn to share the pain. By the power of the Holy Spirit, we can see suffering as a tool to refine faith and strengthen our relationship with God in Jesus Christ.

❖   **Father, strengthen us by Your Holy Spirit so that we do not despair or falter when pressed by trial and tribulation; for Jesus' sake. Amen.**

_____

_____

_____

_____

_____

_____

_____

_____

_____

_____

_____

_____

_____

_____

_____

_____

_____

_____

_____

_____

_____

Painful experiences can leave us angry with God. By the cross, we understand that God loves us and works through everything in our lives for our salvation (Romans 8:28). In Christ alone, we receive full assurance of God's love for us.

❖ **Lord, teach me each day to beg Your pardon and believe Your promise that even amid suffering, You are working for my good. Amen.**

When we are at our lowest, we might agree with Job that there is no hope. If we focus on our pain or problems and look only to ourselves or others for help, we should not be surprised to find only despair. Without a mediator, we face the full wrath of God.

❖ Thank You, heavenly Father, for sending Your Son, our Savior Jesus, to reconcile us to You through the cross and to intercede for us every day (1 John 2:1). Amen.

Our righteousness does not determine our well-being, or lack thereof. Rather, it is all in God's hands. When we become discouraged, it is vital that we remember God's wisdom and power. In Christ "we know that for those who love God all things work together for good" (Romans 8:28).

✦ **Lord, keep us always in this blessed assurance! Amen.**

When we suffer, we tend to see only the anger and condemnation, but we fail to see that God is a God of forgiveness and love. On the cross, Christ suffered not only inscrutable pain physically, emotionally, and mentally for us, but He also suffered hellish spiritual anguish. Through Him we enjoy God's love, now and eternally.

✠ **Almighty God, forgive our many doubts, strengthen our faith, and lead us through this life to the joys of heaven. Amen.**

Regardless of the circumstances and the depth of darkness you may face, call on Jesus Christ, the only mediator between God and all people (1 Timothy 2:5). No matter how bad things may be, Christ is now interceding for you at the right hand of God (Romans 8:34).

❖ **We rejoice, O Father, that Your Son intercedes for us. Hear our plea. Amen.**

Job will receive his vindication in his resurrected body, from which he will see the Redeemer with his own eyes. Today, the Redeemer sees you in your helpless state. As a true Redeemer who buys back His kinsman from bondage, Christ has won you for Himself at the cost of His own flesh and blood.

✤   **Come, Lord Jesus, raise up Your saints! Amen.**

_____

_____

_____

_____

_____

_____

_____

_____

_____

_____

_____

_____

_____

_____

_____

_____

_____

_____

_____

_____

_____

_____

We must look beyond the injustice we observe and continually confess that our outward predicament does not define God's attitude toward us. While the houses of the wicked remain after earthly storms, the spiritual houses of those in Christ endure forever against sin, the world, and the devil because they are built on the rock that is Christ (Matthew 7:24–27).

✤   **Dear Lord Jesus Christ, assure us that nothing will ever take us from Your hands (John 10:28). Amen.**

Job complains that God seemed distant and impossible to find. Yet he remains convinced—by faith and not by sight (2 Corinthians 5:7)—that God does not change His will. Though you suffer poverty and injustice, know that the Lord wills your good and desires your salvation.

❖　**O almighty and merciful Lord, draw near. Answer me gently through Christ Jesus, my Lord. Amen.**

Job's faith in God grows stronger in the face of his difficulties, just as iron is strengthened on the anvil and in the forge. No matter what befalls him, Job entrusts all things to his Creator.

✣   Lord, we know that "by God's power [we] are being guarded through faith for a salvation ready to be revealed in the last time" (1 Peter 1:5). Amen.

Job will learn that God has His purpose in suffering. There is no way for humans to see behind the mask of God, to know God's will apart from Scripture. He reveals His gracious will through the Word, not by reason or experience.

✚ **Set before our eyes Your good and gracious will toward us in the suffering, death, and resurrection of Jesus. Amen.**

_____

_____

_____

_____

_____

_____

_____

_____

_____

_____

_____

_____

_____

_____

_____

_____

_____

_____

_____

_____

_____

When we encounter trials, we can be comforted knowing that God is not punishing us because of our sin, but is strengthening our faith through testing.

✢   **Lord, guide me by the answers of Your Word, and silence the opinions of those who break counsel with You. Amen.**

The Lord uses affliction not just for our punishment but also for our deliverance. Allow affliction to open your ears to learn the Lord's purposes, and to open your mouth in praises. Praise Christ most highly, who delivers you from evil by His agony and bloody sweat.

❖   **O Lord, lay Your hands on the cross, and use that tool for my instruction and deliverance. Amen.**

Like Job, we, too, may become silent before the Lord, but it is often to plan our further defense or to pout in rebellious self-righteousness. How much we miss by trying to justify our own lives! God continues to wait for us and loves us with a never-ending love, which is ours in Christ.

✤ "On Christ, the solid rock, I stand; All other ground is sinking sand." Amen. (*LSB* 575:2)

Job did not accuse his friends and ask for judgment, but followed the Lord's gracious lead and acted as their mediator before the Lord. Jesus, who suffered for us, also pleads for us daily. He is our priestly intercessor and our personal Savior from sin, death, and the devil.

✤ **Lord, teach us the friendly arts of intercession and patience, for You have shown such friendship to us. Amen.**

David pleads with the Lord for deliverance from anxiety, physical discomfort, and sickness caused by a growing awareness of his sinful condition. Nearly 2,000 years ago, our sinful condition was so desperate that God sent His own Son to pay the price. Through faith in Christ's redemption, our sins have been forgiven.

✣ **Lord, hear my plea, and accept my prayer through the merits of Jesus, who prays for me. Amen.**

Our faith is often tested and often found wanting. God's faithfulness and mercy toward us, however, never wanes or fails. He extends His grace audibly and visibly through Word and Sacrament, as a testament of His great and unending love for us.

❖ **O Lord, though we are found wanting for righteousness, save us by the righteousness of Christ. Amen.**

_____

_____

_____

_____

_____

_____

_____

_____

_____

_____

_____

_____

_____

_____

_____

_____

_____

_____

_____

_____

When our prayers question God and His ways, we do well to remember that Jesus not only commanded us to pray but also graciously promised to hear our prayers and intercede for us before the Father. No matter how weak our prayers or deep our frustration, Jesus' grace makes up for their shortcomings.

❖   **Lord Jesus, teach us to know that You are greater than all things, so that we pray confidently, Thy will be done. Amen.**

We may feel alone and forsaken by God. Truly we deserve to be forsaken by Him because of our sinfulness. But Christ truly was forsaken by His Father and died alone so that we could be reconciled to our God. We are never alone because our crucified, resurrected Savior is with us.

✤   **Loving Savior, Your death and resurrection have made us Your people. Lead us to proclaim Your constant care. Amen.**

Human beings are prone to fearful responses. We worry about problems in this life, acting as if we face them alone. Yet God is our light and our salvation. Since He has redeemed us, we have nothing to fear. "If God is for us, who can be against us?" (Romans 8:31).

❖   **O Christ, my light and my salvation, comfort me and strengthen my faith. Amen.**

Sorrowful times in life are sometimes caused by things outside of our control and sometimes by our own sins. Trusting in God's deliverance, David knows that the sorrow he feels will be replaced with joy as God comforts him. We, too, are confident in God's promise to comfort us and dry our tears (Revelation 7:17).

❖　**O God, comfort me with Your presence, and fill me with joy. Amen.**

As saint and sinner, we are unable to keep God's Law perfectly, though He requires that we do so. By the power of His Word and Spirit and by faith, He instills in us a new desire. Our Lord Christ kept the Law perfectly and died on our behalf that we might live with Him in His kingdom.

✤ **O my Lord, preserve me, I earnestly pray, that I will cling truly and solely to You. Amen.**

We as individuals, and as the Church, experience many troubles in this life on account of the devil, the world, and our own sinful nature. Yet amid every crisis of body or soul, God is with us in His Son so that we may face every upheaval.

✤   **O Lord, make us to know You as our refuge and strength, our very present help in every trouble. Amen.**

Sin is an inheritance, born in us, ever damaging us. None of our works can ever set us free from terror, despair, or death. However, God has blotted out even the worst of our sins—adultery and murder—by Jesus' sacrifice.

✜ **Holy Spirit, create me new again, giving joy for sadness. Have mercy on me, O God, and cleanse me from my sin. Amen.**

In times of sudden testing and unexpected trouble, we easily become disillusioned and wonder if God has abandoned us. However, in every trouble, God is our sure helper. The deliverance He provides in Christ, who Himself knew persecution unto death, makes us triumphant despite every appearance to the contrary.

❖   **God, thank You for being my helper, the upholder of my life. Amen.**

When false rumors fly and your reputation suffers, seek divine justice. Turn to the Lord and put the situation in His hands. Do not try to "get even," but leave the outcome to God. Jesus also endured all kinds of plots against His life and slander during His ministry. He knows how to justify you.

❖   **Lord, I exalt in You, my refuge. Amen.**

The psalmist realizes that even the best of the Davidic kings fell short of the ideal. So we also often fail to live as we should. Yet our hope is in David's Son and Lord, Jesus Christ, who has brought us eternal salvation.

✤   **O God, You are great in Your forgiveness. Amen.**

God judges the wicked and delivers the believer according to His timetable, not ours. His seeming delay in this should not cause us to lose heart but to continue in repentance and faith. As He has fulfilled all His promises in the past, so He will act in both judgment and salvation.

✤   **We give thanks to You, O God, and recount Your wondrous deeds. Amen.**

Injustice, weakness, exploitation, continued trial and suffering—such afflictions can make the believer feel isolated and forgotten by God. Your heavenly Father has already judged you impartially by laying all of your sins upon Jesus. This provides you with salvation and endurance, even in the face of worldly injustice.

✢ **Thank You, dear Jesus, that You fully bore the justice that was once due to me. Amen.**

_____

_____

_____

_____

_____

_____

_____

_____

_____

_____

_____

_____

_____

_____

_____

_____

_____

_____

_____

_____

Rather than feeling overwhelmed by the obstacles that confront us, keep the eyes of your faith focused upon the Lord, for He alone is God. Because of the Lord's steadfast love, He cannot overlook or neglect His children. He cannot and will not fail to act according to His mercy and grace.

❖   **Lord, help me and comfort me so that I may enjoy peace of mind and spirit. Amen.**

In worship, you receive the strength of God's steadfast love and faithfulness. No doubt, there are days you wonder if going to worship is worth the effort. But focus on what God has done for you in Jesus, who is faithful to His promises. One day justice will be served on the wicked, but we who believe will flourish in the strength of Christ's resurrection.

❖ **Lord, bring forth praises out of our hearts. Amen.**

The defeats of life are discouraging. Thanks be to God that He is victorious for us! Sin and death are conquered. Satan's head is crushed. Eternally, we are God's children. All creation is waiting for that final day of redemption. For the Lord's victory is an empty tomb on Easter morning.

❖   **Thank You, Lord, for the glorious victory of our salvation, which only You could give us! Amen.**

Despite Israel's persistent disobedience, God consistently upheld His promises and saved them. As we struggle with temptation, we can be sure that God will remain faithful, granting us true repentance and new life in Christ.

❖ **O Lord, You have faithfully saved us through Jesus' obedience, suffering, death, and resurrection. Amen.**

From time to time, old defeats come back to haunt us. Perhaps a future challenge reminds us of a past failure. At times like this, we remember that God, who delivered us in the past, is with us in the present and the future.

❖ O Lord, Satan would remind me of my past failures. Forgive all my sins—past, present, and future. Amen.

We may sometimes wonder, "Where is the steadfast love of God?" He revealed His steadfast love in humble Israel, in the Child of the Virgin Mary. He veiled His greatest gift in what is least among people so that His gift might be received by all.

❖ **O Lord, I know that I do not have to rise up to You, for You have lowered Yourself to save me. Amen.**

God's Word is our beloved guide to life. It reveals God's trustworthy promises and eternal mercy. The Gospel radiates through the psalm as the psalmist describes God's promises, which save His people. God is merciful, and this mercy brings life.

✣ **Lord, give us the faith to believe that all You have said is true and that all Your promises will be fulfilled in Christ. Amen.**

Our strength and safety come only by God's hand. We are in danger from flood and snare, the overwhelming and the enticing. But God is faithful for His name's sake. He rescues us so that we will continue to bless and call on His name.

❖ **Lead us safely, Lord, so we may always give glory to Your name. Amen.**

_____

_____

_____

_____

_____

_____

_____

_____

_____

_____

_____

_____

_____

_____

_____

_____

_____

_____

_____

_____

_____

If we are honest with ourselves, we must admit the depths of our sinfulness. When we are overwhelmed, God hears our pleas for mercy. He does not remember our sins, but rather grants us free forgiveness through the work of Christ, who gives us hope.

❖   **O Lord, in our weakness we find Your strength. Speak to us the word of Your promise. Amen.**

We know that sin brings regret, grief, self-loathing, and bitterness. (Such emotions are signs of repentance.) Yet we can also look for our deliverance, clinging to God's promises of redemption delivered by one wholly innocent, Jesus, God's own Child.

❖ **O Lord, deliver us from our captivity to sin, through Your Son, Jesus Christ. Amen.**

_____

_____

_____

_____

_____

_____

_____

_____

_____

_____

_____

_____

_____

_____

_____

_____

_____

_____

_____

_____

_____

_____

Our sins isolate us from others. We are shut out of the community of the righteous. Jesus Christ, more than anyone, was persecuted, deserted, imprisoned, and tormented. But His Father raised Him from the dead to live in the company of those made righteous through His blood.

✣   **Heavenly Father, be my defender, my refuge, my portion in Christ. Amen.**

Everything that breathes should praise the Lord because of His mighty deeds and His "excellent greatness"! Of the many reasons to praise God, for us the most joyous are "His mighty deeds" (v. 2) by which He has redeemed us in Christ and brought us to faith.

✚　**O Lord, may the praises in the Psalms, the praises in the Church, and the praises in heaven equip me to join in praising You! Amen.**

Solomon's introduction reminds us of the difference between true wisdom and the wisdom of the world. True wisdom is from the Lord, a message that is foolishness to those who reject it but God's very power to us who are being saved (1 Corinthians 1:18).

❖   **Lord, teach us true wisdom and give us its power to love and serve You. Amen.**

Godly parents warn their children of the temporal and eternal consequences of wickedness. The heavenly Father assures us of the grace and blessings God offers to those who love and trust in their Savior and who, relying on His Spirit's power, seek to walk in His light.

❖   **Lord, Help us correctly and appropriately to teach others of Your will and love. Amen.**

Proverbs teaches us to weigh the heavy consequences of sexual immorality before we act. Personal health, reputation, family, and career are at stake—and our relationship with God. Wisdom, who is Jesus Christ, brings us the power and motivation to live worthy of our holy calling.

❖ **Father, give me the wisdom to walk away from temptation and to overcome it by Your Word and Spirit. Amen.**

DATE

TOPICS

Proverbs 7:1–27

The one who commits adultery chooses immediate gratification over faithfully keeping one's commitments to God and spouse. Christ, the One who is faithful in all things, offers forgiveness for all who have taken this deadly turn. God's Word and wisdom light the way to sexual purity and marital faithfulness.

✢ **Lord Jesus, be for me the way that leads from death to life. Amen.**

296

The Lord is our Wisdom. Christ calls us from worldly foolishness, judgment, and death to obedience, God's favor, and abundant life. He reaches out in love to all who love Him and diligently seek Him. In Christ, our Wisdom, we are rich beyond any human measure!

✤　**Lord, make us wise unto Your salvation, that by Your gracious wisdom we may truly live. Amen.**

God's Law warns against the deadly foolishness all around us. Life in the Gospel saves us from a naive gullibility that sets us up for moral and spiritual disaster. The folly of sin gets a just punishment—death. The wisdom of our God-given faith brings eternal life.

✤   **Lord, save me from the folly of going my own way, for in the end folly abandons me in the company of the dead. Amen.**

Both the righteous and the wicked face tempests and challenges. Yet the righteous, who travel the way of the Lord and who live in the fear of the Lord, are blessed with stability, joy, and the promise of everlasting life. The Lord is your hope, health, stronghold, and way.

❖ **Lord Jesus, keep us from straying from the path You have set before us, and renew our hope in You. Amen.**

Worldly logic tells us that we become wealthy by hoarding what we have. But God's Word tells us that true riches come to those who give generously. God has generously given us all that we need, including the life of His one and only Son for our salvation.

❖ **Lord, we rejoice in the great blessings You have given us. Amen.**

The foolish are gullible and believe everything. They are reckless, careless, and quick-tempered. But because wise people thoughtfully evaluate everything on the basis of God's Word, their words and actions are always prudent and cautious.

❖   **Lord God, lead us to walk by faith, always expressing ourselves with the gentleness and self-control that come from You. Amen.**

_____

Stop gossip before it begins, not only by defending the one spoken about but also by calling the gossiper to repentance and safeguarding ourselves from what may do irreparable damage. What joy it would be if we let our Lord's forgiveness teach us to be as silent about the sins and shortcomings of our neighbor as God is pleased to be toward ours for Jesus' sake!

❖ **Heavenly Father, teach us to keep both our lips and our ears from the evil that may be spoken of others. Amen.**

Children are born fools, since they are born sinful. No one should abandon them to their sinfulness but nurture and admonish them through God's Word. God's dear Son became a fool for our sakes, pierced and lashed to rescue us from foolishness and to deliver us to God.

❖ O Father, welcome me now—Your prodigal child—for Brother Jesus has borne the blows and strokes of my cleansing. Amen.

Folly is an act of rebellion against God. True wisdom flows out of trust in the Lord. By putting our trust in God and in His Son—Jesus Christ, Wisdom in human flesh—we are delivered from the consequences of our folly and we grow in the righteous behavior marked by wisdom.

❖ **Dear heavenly Father, forgive us for the many ways that we have shown the folly of our hearts. Amen.**

_____

_____

_____

_____

_____

_____

_____

_____

_____

_____

_____

_____

_____

_____

_____

_____

_____

_____

_____

_____

_____

_____

Solomon knows that true piety is more than simply avoiding evil but is based on trust in God. Thus, he urges us not to envy sinners but to fear the Lord, for the Lord has graciously promised us a glorious future (23:17–18; 24:1–4, 13–14).

❖ **Lord, may we be moved to grow in godliness, while ever remembering that true righteousness is ours through Christ alone. Amen.**

We are to engage in the sort of decent conduct that enables societies to flourish. While all societies recognize the value of these behaviors, we Christians seek to live in such ways because the Gospel frees us to serve our neighbors in a God-pleasing way.

❖ **Heavenly Father, grant us justice, honesty, and industrious service. Through Christ's death and resurrection change our hearts and our society. Amen.**

Righteous people who compromise their principles disappoint us. Hope remains not in the possibility of them renewing their righteousness but rather in God's righteousness, which frees, strengthens, and moves us to pursue what can be called "active" righteousness by keeping the Law to thank the Lord for His mercy.

❖ **Lord, refresh us this day with the faithful message of Your love that we may search out what is pleasing to You. Amen.**

The righteousness of rulers and their subjects is borne out of the divine righteousness reckoned to human beings through faith in God's promises. The righteousness that saves is a righteousness that only comes through faith in God's promise; Christ's righteousness was substituted for our wickedness.

❖ **We thank You, O Lord, for Your greatest act of justice, the sending of Your own Son to die on our behalf! Amen.**

_____

_____

_____

_____

_____

_____

_____

_____

_____

_____

_____

_____

_____

_____

_____

_____

_____

_____

_____

_____

_____

We cannot obtain enough insight, correct every injustice, or curb some of the most common sins. It is only through knowledge of the Holy One— God's only Son, Jesus Christ, who was crucified, died, and resurrected— that we are rescued from pressure of inadequacy, failure, and, ultimately, eternal damnation.

✧   **O Lord, raise us up in newness of life, so that we may love and serve our neighbors. Amen.**

Our lives, no matter how well lived, will not win favor in God's sight on the Last Day. Life is fleeting and has no meaning apart from God's love in Christ Jesus. Faith worked in us by the power of the Gospel brings meaning to life and the certainty of forgiveness, life, and salvation.

✥   **Lord God, grant us a right understanding that we might always rejoice in Christ's salvation. Amen.**

_____

_____

_____

_____

_____

_____

_____

_____

_____

_____

_____

_____

_____

_____

_____

_____

_____

_____

_____

_____

_____

_____

Do not regard the accolades and accoutrements of the world as more important than the Lord and His gracious gifts. Though we continually search for contentment in this "under the sun" existence, Christ is our eternal Lord and King of kings.

❖   **Dear God and Father, thank You for Your infinite goodness and love toward us. Amen.**

What person is better for his or her wealth, pleasure, and honor when standing before God at the final judgment? Jesus Christ is the way and the truth and the life (John 14:6; Acts 4:12). He is the author and perfecter of our faith, so that we do not grow weary and lose heart (cf. Hebrews 12:2–3).

✤   **O God of all comfort, grant us a firm, glad, and grateful faith, that by it we may overcome every trial. Amen.**

Although we see others getting away with doing wrong, we should not follow them. Instead, we should continue to follow God's will and commit ourselves to His judgments, which will be favorable to the believer in the end.

✤   **God, grant us patience as we see the temporary successes of the ungodly. Remind us of the final outcome You have prepared for us in Christ. Amen.**

It appears unfair that all people must die, as death deals equally with evil people as well as those who follow God. We need something to counter the hopelessness that there is nothing after death. For that reason, God comforts us with His promises of love and mercy.

❖   **Thank You, God, that Your promises, fulfilled in Christ, give us the sure and certain hope of being with You forever. Amen.**

_____

_____

_____

_____

_____

_____

_____

_____

_____

_____

_____

_____

_____

_____

_____

_____

_____

_____

_____

_____

To avoid a meaningless life, one needs a right relationship with God, i.e., justification based on God's favor toward us on account of Christ and received through faith. Thought God's Word, we can know Him and how to avoid a meaningless life now and in eternity.

❖ **Heavenly Father, thank You for already judging me as worthy of life through the death and resurrection of Your Son, our Savior. Amen.**

The Shulammite is easily despised, but she is the love of her husband-king. The Church, too, is the beloved of our Bridegroom, Christ Jesus. Her sins may be obvious, even to other sinners, but her Husband-King calls her holy and forgiven in the glory of His grace.

❖   **Lord, lead us not to judge ourselves or one another by outward appearance, but to listen to Your Word, which calls us God-pleasing in Your sight, for Jesus' sake. Amen.**

_____

_____

_____

_____

_____

_____

_____

_____

_____

_____

_____

_____

_____

_____

_____

_____

_____

_____

_____

_____

_____

Like Solomon calling the Shulammite, our Lord calls us to come out of our worldliness and to reside in communion with Him. He calls us holy, beautiful, stainless, pure. He calls us forgiven in His Gospel.

✤   **Lord, teach us how much You love us, how beautiful we are in Your eyes, how washed, how clean, how holy and pure. Amen.**

We are not to conform ourselves to the pattern of this world, but remain holy, set apart as a wall (v. 10). The Lord wants to preserve His dear ones till the end.

❖ **Come, Jesus, fill the hearts of Your faithful, and kindle in them the fire of Your love. Stir up our hearts that at Your second coming we may worship You in purity and in truth. Amen.**

The Lord describes His wrath against idolatry. Like Judah, many lands today are filled with idols (wealth, power, beauty, and fascination with new religions). These cannot compare to the true God, who is powerful to judge and to save as He will when Christ returns.

❖   **Return, O Lord, and deliver us from our self-destructive ways. Grant us satisfaction in Your goodness. Amen.**

The Lord prophesies that Judah will suffer due to a lack of sound leadership, despite its current prosperity. No matter how great the wealth you amass, the risk of loss is unavoidable. Invest in the true source of security and contentment: the Lord.

✤ **Jesus, cover me in the robe of Your righteousness. Grant me honest shame and true repentance. Amen.**

___

___

___

___

___

___

___

___

___

___

___

___

___

___

___

___

___

___

___

___

___

___

___

Today, popular culture longs to be "bad," and our "heroes" corrupt basic morality. Reject the excuses of pop culture and instead revel in the community of faith, which knows right from wrong. The Lord our Counsel will guide us to true joy and lasting pleasure in the goodness of life.

❖   **Lord, snap the tethers of sin that hold me back and rob me of genuine freedom in Christ. Amen.**

Throughout history, and in your life, the Lord works in two basic ways: Law and Gospel. Unlike Israel, walk in these ways daily, confessing your sins and asking His forgiveness. Though He chastens you, He will restore you through Jesus, the holy Seed.

✣ **O Lord, may the root of Your goodness spring forth in my life. Amen.**

_____

_____

_____

_____

_____

_____

_____

_____

_____

_____

_____

_____

_____

_____

_____

_____

_____

_____

_____

_____

_____

Judah would be all but swept away by Assyria. Yet the Lord would still abide with and protect His people. The Lord abides with us still, even amid judgment and devastation. He is our Immanuel, and nothing can sweep Him away.

❖ **Merciful Lord, defend me even as You chasten me. Lead me to sincere confession and enduring faith. Amen.**

The Holy One, the Lord God of hosts, will always welcome our repentance and turn our hearts toward Him. Just as the Lord had pity on Judah and Israel, preserving a remnant, He will have pity on His people (the Church) today.

✠   **O Lord, deliver us from false saviors who would rob us of Your blessings given through Christ, our Lord. Amen.**

_____

_____

_____

_____

_____

_____

_____

_____

_____

_____

_____

_____

_____

_____

_____

_____

_____

_____

_____

_____

_____

The Lord describes the coming rule of the Messiah. As believers in Christ, we already enjoy the benefits of His wise rule, having received His Spirit, wisdom, peace, and other blessings. The Spirit equips us to spread word of this blessed reign to all nations.

✤   **Pour out Your sevenfold Spirit, O Lord, that we may boldly proclaim Your goodness. Amen.**

The fall of Babylon's king is a warning to never put ourselves in the place of God. While the glorious king of Babylon remained in the grave, our King, the Lord Jesus Christ, rose from the grave. Through faith in Him, our guilt is taken away, and our resurrection is assured.

✟   **Lord God, even as we are surrounded by the anger and wickedness of the powerful, give us comfort and joy in knowing that You have destroyed death for us. Amen.**

God's own people would experience His wrath, for they had lived in ways indistinguishable from the nations. When we do not live lives of repentance, we are also indistinguishable from unbelievers. We are called to drown our old Adam by daily contrition and repentance.

✠   **Lord, lead us each day in the glad confidence that You have atoned for our iniquity and opened the kingdom of heaven for us. Amen.**

We stand before God as poor, miserable sinners. Although we deserve to suffer for our guilt, we can sing for joy that the Righteous One, Jesus Christ, has suffered in our place. "He was wounded for our transgressions; He was crushed for our iniquities" (53:5).

✤   **Gracious Lord, we praise and glorify You for the salvation You have accomplished for us through Your dear Son, Jesus Christ, the Righteous One. Amen.**

We should always recognize that earthly authorities are only mortals through whom the Lord works on behalf of His people. Through His death and resurrection, Jesus has accomplished the salvation of sinners. His work guarantees that our bodies will also rise.

✣   **Lord Jesus, grant to us the perfect peace that is found only through faith in You. Amen.**

Like the people of Jerusalem, we are often tempted to take refuge in pleasant-sounding lies. Instead, we should gladly learn the wonderful counsel of God's Word. Jesus is God's promised and precious cornerstone. Whoever believes and builds on this foundation will find the power of sin and death annulled.

❖ **Lord, open our ears always to give attention to Your Word, that we may find refuge in Your wonderful counsel. Amen.**

After a time of destruction, the Lord will be gracious to His people, binding them up and healing them in mercy. In adversity, we learn to walk in the way of the Lord and hear His Word. He has been merciful to all by sending His Son. In Jesus, the Father gives His people healing from the brokenness of our sin.

✤　**Gracious Lord, open our eyes to see You, and give us faith to wait for You in quiet confidence. Amen.**

A coming king will reign in righteousness, opening the eyes and ears of God's people. We should give attention to what the Lord has revealed and speak His truth distinctly. Jesus is our King who reigns in righteousness and shares that righteousness with all who believe in Him, providing them with shelter from the storms of sin and death.

❖ **King of Righteousness, keep our hearts free from iniquity and error and busy with the noble things You desire. Amen.**

_____

_____

_____

_____

_____

_____

_____

_____

_____

_____

_____

_____

_____

_____

_____

_____

_____

_____

_____

_____

The Lord prepares the salvation of His exiled people. Today, no matter what foolishness or fear has snared you, confess your sins in the confidence that the Lord has redeemed you by grace alone and has prepared for you a new way of life.

✤ **Take my trembling hand, Lord Jesus, and lead me to the comforts of Zion. Amen.**

The Lord rebukes Hezekiah for expressing hope in Babylon as his ally against Assyria. Prayer is our ever-ready strength, and the Lord is our ever-present ally. When worries assault you, call on the Lord. His Son will rule for your benefit and deliver you peace.

✤ **Turn all my doubts, O Lord, into prayers, that I may see a secure future for Your servants. Amen.**

The Lord lowers the nations but prepares for Israel's restoration. Today, follow where the Lord leads, according to the teachings of His Word. He will take you by the hand and walk with you to clear the way, so great is His mercy in Christ.

✣ **Lord Jesus, at the Father's right hand, sanctify me and guide my steps, that I walk like Abraham, Your friend. Amen.**

Israel fails to believe and live as God's servant, and is punished with exile. No person should seek security in his own righteousness, for we are delivered for the sake of the Lord's righteousness alone. He calls us and delivers us according to His righteous purposes.

✦ **Lord, magnify Your Word in my seeing and hearing, that I may serve You in righteousness. Amen.**

_____

_____

_____

_____

_____

_____

_____

_____

_____

_____

_____

_____

_____

_____

_____

_____

_____

_____

_____

_____

_____

The Lord prophesies the restoration of His people, centuries before the events take place. Today, despite the difficulties that beset you, the Lord holds your future securely. In fact, He planned for your future through His beloved Son.

✣   **O Redeemer, I entrust all my days to Your care. Fulfill Your purpose for me. Amen.**

The Babylonians regard themselves as uniquely wise and blessed through their astrological devotion, but they will be enslaved and humiliated. If you put your confidence in astrology, horoscopes, incantations, or charms, you will fall too. True wisdom comes from the Lord and His Word. He gives His blessings through the Word and in answer to prayer.

✤ **O Lord, grant me wisdom in making decisions and contentment in the blessings I receive. Amen.**

Isaiah prophesies Israel's return and prosperity in contrast with the humiliation of the oppressors. Today, regard your sins with appropriate shame, but likewise see that the Lord, your Savior, has redeemed you. He will not forget you. He longs to restore you and your family.

✤ **Jesus, the memorials of my salvation are graven on Your palms. Show them to all as a sign of Your mercy and forgiveness toward me and all sinners. Amen.**

The Lord contrasts His Servant's humility and obedience with Israel's rebelliousness. The Servant's obedience and suffering atoned for your sins and the sins of all the world. Walk in the light of His Word. In Him there is no disgrace.

✢   Awaken my ear, O Jesus. Rouse me each day to fear, love, and trust my Lord. Amen.

_____

_____

_____

_____

_____

_____

_____

_____

_____

_____

_____

_____

_____

_____

_____

_____

_____

_____

_____

In this final Servant Song (52:13–53:12), the Lord sacrifices the innocent Servant for the sake of ignorant, rebellious transgressors, making atonement for them. Commit this passage to heart. Few places in Scripture describe God's surpassing mercy for you in so touching a manner.

❖ "What wondrous love is this That caused the Lord of bliss To bear the dreadful curse for my soul, for my soul, To bear the dreadful curse for my soul!" Amen. (*LSB* 543:1)

DATE

TOPICS

We often pursue personal pleasure and gain at the expense of our God-given responsibilities. Unlike Israel's leaders who sought their own gain, Jesus is our Good Shepherd. He laid down His life for every sinful sheep, faithfully fulfilling God's righteous requirements for our sake.

✤ **Give us grace, dear Lord, to follow You always in the way that leads to life everlasting. Amen.**

_____

_____

_____

_____

_____

_____

_____

_____

_____

_____

_____

_____

_____

_____

_____

_____

_____

_____

_____

_____

_____

We are not righteous enough to achieve salvation by our own merits. In mercy, Christ Jesus has interceded on our behalf. His zeal is for our salvation, which He made possible through His suffering, death, and resurrection. His perfect righteousness is freely given to all who believe.

❖ **Merciful Redeemer, grant that by Your Word and Spirit we might turn from our transgression and always rejoice in the gift of Your salvation. Amen.**

As brokenhearted souls, we must confess the sinful cause of our poverty and brokenness. Jesus brings liberty for all held captive by sin and death. By His death and resurrection, He has delivered us from the shame of our sin, clothed us in His own righteousness, and made us to be His holy priests.

✢ **Lord God, lead us to be comforted each day in Your robe of righteousness. Amen.**

_____

_____

_____

_____

_____

_____

_____

_____

_____

_____

_____

_____

_____

_____

_____

_____

_____

_____

_____

_____

The Lord will bring about a new birth of joy and delight. We should not look elsewhere for lasting satisfaction and comfort. Just as a child's mother meets his or her needs, so our heavenly Father meets our needs of provision and pardon.

❖ **Gracious Lord, by Your Son, Jesus Christ, You delivered us from destruction. Carry us and bless us with the comfort and peace that only You can give. Amen.**

God sent prophets like Jeremiah to convict His people of their sin so that they might repent and return to Him. In mercy, God patiently waited, providing ample time for repentance. He is likewise patient toward you, whom He calls to repentance and true faith in Christ.

✤ **Father, I thank You for the Law to reveal my sin and guide my conduct, and the Gospel to show me the Savior and Your love through Him. Amen.**

Like a hurricane-force wind, Babylon's armies will sweep Judah away, leaving only a few survivors. God had sent prophet after prophet to warn His people and call them to repentance because He loved them and wanted them back. Today, He calls you so that you may receive His gracious salvation.

❖ **Father, turn us from our foolish ways to walk by faith in Your Word, through Jesus Christ. Amen.**

God rejects sacrifices offered without faith; He is not satisfied with token compliance. Instead, He calls us to repent and to live our faith in all we say and do. Despite our faithless acts, God continues to be faithful through His Son, Jesus, our Savior.

❖   **Open our eyes, Father, and send us Your Spirit, that we live our lives for You, avoiding sin and helping others. Amen.**

_____

_____

_____

_____

_____

_____

_____

_____

_____

_____

_____

_____

_____

_____

_____

_____

_____

_____

_____

_____

_____

Although it breaks His heart, God must punish unrepentant sinners because He is just and righteous. Yet the Lord yearns to forgive His people. Today, repent and turn to Him with all your heart. Though the Lord's testing is painful, He promises to refine you through Christ.

❖　**O Lord, lead us every day to live our faith in thought, word, and deed, through Jesus Christ. Amen.**

Like scarecrows, idols are inanimate objects crafted by human hands. They have no power to harm or to help. God is all-powerful, so no one can escape His justice and judgment. Yet God is so great, He can also do the impossible: save sinners without violating His own righteousness (cf. Romans 3:21–26).

✤ **Turn our eyes and hearts, O Lord, from the worthless vanities of this world to You, through Jesus Christ. Amen.**

_____

_____

_____

_____

_____

_____

_____

_____

_____

_____

_____

_____

_____

_____

_____

_____

_____

_____

Often we are unable to understand God's justice or reconcile God's providence with the evil we experience. Own sense of right and wrong gets terribly twisted by sin. Yet take heart. God continually works in the world for justice and for the salvation of people, something He guarantees by the cross of Christ.

❖ **Teach us to be patient, Lord, when we do not understand "why." Amen.**

Jeremiah expresses his frustration over false prophets who tell the people that peace lies ahead, though Jeremiah has warned them that destruction is coming. People need to know they are sinners, condemned by God's Law. Then, crushed by the Law, the repentant sinner is ready for the Gospel, the healing Word of God that grants abiding peace.

✤   **Lead us to share Your Word faithfully, O Lord, and bear witness to Your grace in Jesus Christ. Amen.**

Persistent sin can only result in condemnation by God and loss of all joy. God alone will provide strength for Jeremiah in his difficult ministry, just as He provides all we need in Jesus Christ. He is the blessed Bridegroom for His beloved Bride, the Church.

❖ **Strengthen us, O Lord, to do Your will, and bring all parts of our lives into harmony with our faith in Jesus Christ. Amen.**

The Judeans' rejection of God is plainly seen in their mistreatment of His prophet Jeremiah. Those who proclaim God's Word faithfully will likely face persecution. Yet believers stand in grace, confident of God's love. He makes us a new creation just as a potter reworks a lump of clay.

❖   **Anchor us in Christ crucified, O Lord, and keep us faithful to You. Shape our lives through Jesus, our Savior. Amen.**

People worship wealth and power today, sacrificing integrity and compassion for temporary riches. Jesus, having all things, avoids the deceit of wealth and power (Matthew 4:8–10), remaining faithful to the plan of salvation by going to the cross to save us from our sinful deceptions.

❖ **Lord, faithful Shepherd, lead us to treasure people more than things. Amen.**

God promises to give His people a new and righteous King who will save and protect them as long as He reigns over them. Jesus, the Good Shepherd, is this King, and He draws all believers together in one flock of faith, laying down His life for them and taking it up again (John 10).

✤ **Dear Jesus, keep us in Your flock, safe from all harm and danger. Amen.**

Idolatry and immorality, including abuse and neglect of the poor, will be severely punished in the end. Ultimately, Jesus pays for the sins of all people and every nation by His death on the cross. Throughout these warnings to the nations, God's promise of a Savior continues to shine through.

✧   **Father, may Your Gospel go forth for all nations. Amen.**

Jeremiah warns the populace of Jerusalem that the worst is yet to come. The wages of sin is death (Romans 6:23a). However, God does not delight in punishing sinners. He also sends true prophets and faithful ministers to turn people from death to life—God's gift to us in Christ Jesus (Romans 6:23b).

✤ **Teach us, Lord, to avoid sin and wait upon Your Word, that we may have life in Jesus Christ. Amen.**

_____

_____

_____

_____

_____

_____

_____

_____

_____

_____

_____

_____

_____

_____

_____

_____

_____

_____

_____

_____

_____

Pray that the Lord would guide your words and deeds as you care for those entrusted to your leadership in family, church, or society. Take heart, knowing that God's Word prevails, stronger than any opposing force, and it accomplishes its purpose: your salvation.

✣   **Keep us steadfast in Your Word of truth, O Lord. Amen.**

Surrounded by the enemy army, it may have seemed foolish for Jeremiah to buy land for the future, but obeying God is always the right thing to do. When trouble surrounds you, cling to the Lord's commands and promises. In His mercy, God will save His people and bring them to safety, a promise ultimately fulfilled in Jesus Christ.

❖ **Lord, help us look past the present trouble to see with joy and confidence our eternal home in Jesus Christ. Amen.**

_____

_____

_____

_____

_____

_____

_____

_____

_____

_____

_____

_____

_____

_____

_____

_____

_____

_____

_____

_____

Eventually, the Lord will restore the fortunes of His people, and the empty streets will once again ring with joy and laughter. God's discipline must work itself out at this point before He will show mercy to His rebellious people. God plans a wonderful future for His people, ultimately fulfilled in Christ Jesus.

❖ **Strengthen us, O Lord, in trial and temptation. Keep our eyes on Christ and on our heavenly home. Amen.**

The rich once more enslave the servants they had freed, revealing the unbelief and rebellion at the heart of God's people. Still, God does not reject them forever; He plans for their discipline and restoration. He is faithful to all His promises. To free us, He sent Christ, who is ever faithful.

❖   **Teach us, O Lord, to see others as You see them—through the eyes of Christ Jesus, our Savior. Amen.**

_____

_____

_____

_____

_____

_____

_____

_____

_____

_____

_____

_____

_____

_____

_____

_____

_____

_____

_____

_____

The world hates God and His Word and opposes those who proclaim its truth. However, God does not ignore the plight of His persecuted people, and He will not neglect you. Though you enter the kingdom of heaven through tribulation, your future is assured through the Gospel of God's beloved Son.

✣ **Lord, keep us faithful to Jesus and focused on the prize of eternal life. Amen.**

Like Jeremiah, God's people today should never give up hope but rather trust in the Lord, especially when things are at their worst. Also, God works through us to help one another in time of need, as Jesus helps us in our greatest need by rescuing us from sin and damnation.

❖ **When all seems lost, O Lord, lift up our heads. Keep our hearts faithful and our eyes on You. Amen.**

_____

_____

_____

_____

_____

_____

_____

_____

_____

_____

_____

_____

_____

_____

_____

_____

_____

_____

_____

_____

_____

God does not want His people to place their confidence in Pharaoh or his army. Today, when you face questions in life, seek the Lord's will through the wisdom of His Word and by commending your life to Him through prayer. He will watch over you faithfully and be with you always.

❖   **Help us, heavenly Father, to trust in You above all earthly reason, might, and power. Amen.**

The Judean refugees who fled to Egypt refuse to give up their idolatry. Sadly, mankind often seeks religions that promise prosperity or personal gratification. These are nothing more than self-centered substitutes for faith. True faith comes only through the faithful proclamation of God's lasting treasure—eternal life through Jesus Christ.

❖   **Father, do not let the deceitful wealth of the world tempt us away from You and our Savior Jesus Christ. Amen.**

No matter how strong or powerful God's enemies are, they all fall in the end. God's victory over opposing forces accomplishes two things: (1) it shows God's power over the gods of defeated nations, with the purpose of their salvation; (2) it means life and salvation for His people.

❖ **Lord, may we always see Your loving hand guiding all nations toward eternal salvation, regardless of how hopeless times may seem. Amen.**

During the process of Babylon's destruction, the Israelites will come together to seek the Lord to make an everlasting covenant (vv. 4–5). God's heart aches when the people He loves turn away from Him. Like the father of the prodigal (Luke 15:21–24), He yearns to forgive those who return to Him with repentant hearts.

❖ **Father, lead us by Your Holy Spirit to repentance, and forgive us through Your Son, Jesus Christ. Amen.**

_____

_____

_____

_____

_____

_____

_____

_____

_____

_____

_____

_____

_____

_____

_____

_____

_____

_____

_____

_____

_____

Jeremiah concludes on a hopeful note. Despite Judah's rebellion, God never forgot His promises. Years later, God sent Jesus Christ as the atoning sacrifice for the world's sin. All of God's promises find their Yes in Christ (2 Corinthians 1:20).

✣ **Lead us by Your Holy Spirit, heavenly Father, that we remain faithful to our eternal King, Jesus Christ. Amen.**

Contrasted with the wealth and beauty of its former days, the ruins of Jerusalem lie as a testimony to God's just response against persistent sin and rebellion. But even in the face of His people's faithlessness, God proves Himself faithful to His promise of a Savior by preserving a remnant that will return to Jerusalem.

✠ **Teach us to live wisely, O Lord, according to Your will and in the joy of our salvation in Jesus Christ. Amen.**

_____

_____

_____

_____

_____

_____

_____

_____

_____

_____

_____

_____

_____

_____

_____

_____

_____

_____

_____

_____

_____

The people of Jerusalem have been crushed but not utterly destroyed—their hope must be in the Lord and His great love for them. We are often our own worst enemies, responsible for our suffering through our own choices. No matter how bad things get, our hope is always in the Lord because He loves us in Jesus Christ and never abandons us.

❖   **Lord, do not treat us as our sins deserve, but forgive and restore us to Your unfailing love through Jesus Christ. Amen.**

Lamenting in anguish, God's people appeal to the Lord for forgiveness and restoration. In our own lives, we easily forget God and our calling as His people at times when it seems that everything is going our way. God stands ready to forgive penitent sinners by restoring His blessing to us through the blood of Jesus Christ.

❖ **Father, keep us faithful in good times and secure in our faith during bad times, for we are Yours at all times. Amen.**

Our life may be one of lamentation, mourning, and woe, but that may be the only way to break through pride and lead us to see how hopeless our natural condition is. If, however, God's accusing message is ingested, His word of forgiveness in Christ's atonement will be "as sweet as honey."

❖ **Lord, drown our stubbornness daily in Baptism and raise us with Christ that we may gladly perform the service He gives us. Amen.**

Because God loves deeply, He responds vigorously to those who violate His covenant. The outpouring of His wrath on obstinate unbelievers reminds us that He operates by the same principle in salvation; His Son bore the wrath our sins deserved. His love is costly—a price we could never pay—complete holiness.

✣   **Lord, help us live a holy life that honors Your gift of Your own Son, who paid the price through His blood. Amen.**

All of us constantly stand at the edge of the void, with the devil, the world, and our flesh ever-active and formidable enemies before whom we can never hope to stand by our own resources. Thanks be to God there is a day of mercy, too, which Ezekiel will proclaim and we may celebrate with joy in Christ, our Savior.

❖   **Father, safely usher us through the grave to rest with Christ, and finally, to resurrection and eternal life. Amen.**

A remnant, those bearing a mark of salvation on their foreheads, will escape. The road to perdition is broad, but God does not fail to place His mark of salvation on all who repent, "who sigh and groan over all the abominations that are committed" in the holy city (9:4).

❖   **Lord, help us ward off the temptations to follow the heedless masses who ignore and reject Your Word. Amen.**

_____

_____

_____

_____

_____

_____

_____

_____

_____

_____

_____

_____

_____

_____

_____

_____

_____

_____

_____

_____

_____

Ezekiel is assured that a remnant will be saved. The glory then leaves the city for the Mount of Olives to the east. This is the final judgment upon those who remain in Jerusalem below. Thanks be to God; He gives us His Word and Spirit, new hearts, and new lives in His promises of mercy.

✣   **Lord, send Your Spirit upon us that we remain faithful until death and share in the return of the glory on the Last Day. Amen.**

All religions do not lead to the same place. There is only one true Gospel of salvation by grace through faith in Christ; anyone who preaches or practices otherwise is condemned. By repeating phrases such as "My people," the Lord expresses His offer of salvation to all who believe.

✧   **Lord, keep us firm in the faith until the day of our Lord. Amen.**

Jerusalem is a vine that is good for nothing but burning, a vivid illustration of the city's fall in 587 BC. By this catastrophe, the Lord prepares the way for restoration and salvation. In Christ, the true vine, we can bear much fruit (John 15:1–11).

✣   **Spare us, O Lord, as inhabitants of the new Jerusalem, from the defection and destruction of the old Jerusalem, that in Christ we may finally enter the Jerusalem above. Amen.**

Forgetting God's unmerited grace, Jerusalem chases after the favors of idolatrous nations. God has no alternative but to punish her severely. If the Lord can restore someone who has fallen as far as Jerusalem, He can restore anyone. His grace is broad enough to cover even your greatest sin.

✤ **Lord, keep us ever mindful of all the undeserved mercies You have showered upon us from birth. Amen.**

God gives a clear, almost dogmatic, statement of how His justice operates. Life or death depends upon whether or not one believes and, as a result, lives out that faith. God severely condemns natural man's tendency to justify himself on the basis of his own supposed righteousness, or to blame God (or someone else) for unfairness.

❖ **Lord, keep us steadfast in Christ's righteousness, which has satisfied Your justice and has given us new lives. Amen.**

God will use the Babylonian captivity to bring Israel back into a covenant agreement with Himself. When difficulties or even disasters enter your life, let them remind you of the need for daily repentance and the refreshing blessings of the Gospel extended to you through Christ.

✤   **Merciful Father, forgive my sins and restore me to a right relationship through Your Son, Jesus Christ. Amen.**

_____

_____

_____

_____

_____

_____

_____

_____

_____

_____

_____

_____

_____

_____

_____

_____

_____

_____

_____

God's use of sexually explicit language calls attention to His wrath against spiritual adultery. Today, repent of lusts and from spiritual adulteries that mix true devotion with falsehood. No matter how deep the stain of your sins, trust that the Lord Jesus can cleanse you with His precious blood and renew positive relationships with heaven and at home.

✣ **Father, forgive us for foolishly bowing to our own lusts and sinful imaginations. Amen.**

God calls for true sorrow and contrition as genuine results of repentance. Our sins profaned His most glorious temple—the body and life of His Son. Yet the Father quietly gave Him over to death so that we might have life. Jesus cleanses our pain-filled hearts and will wipe away all our tears.

✣   **O Jesus, when our sin profaned the temple of Your body, You prepared for us a place in Your eternal glory. Return and deliver us. Amen.**

Mocking the Lord brings His retribution. People who pride themselves on criticizing and persecuting God's people will suffer His wrath here or in the grave. Yet, there is hope and beauty for the repentant. Though Tyre would sink down, those who trust the Lord will rise up in blessing.

❖   **Lord, protect us by Your Holy Spirit, through Christ. Amen.**

God directs Israel back to His covenant with their namesake Jacob—
"Israel" (Genesis 28:13–15; 32:28). God's mercy provides a recurring theme
throughout the Bible. His promises point to the cross, where He willingly
sacrificed His Son—the ultimate judgment against sin and the fullness of
our redemption.

❖　**Lord, You are faithful; through Baptism, You have called us
out of sin into eternal life. Amen.**

———————————————————

———————————————————

———————————————————

———————————————————

———————————————————

———————————————————

———————————————————

———————————————————

———————————————————

———————————————————

———————————————————

———————————————————

———————————————————

———————————————————

———————————————————

———————————————————

———————————————————

———————————————————

———————————————————

———————————————————

———————————————————

Just as the strength or weakness of Pharaoh and Nebuchadnezzar were a matter for God's judgment, your life and future are in God's hands. Pray that He would bless and guide the work of your hands today. Note that, through the trembling arms and nail-pierced hands of Jesus, the Lord accomplished His greatest work of salvation.

❖ **Heavenly Father, uphold the hands of Your servant in the cause of righteousness. Amen.**

Today, God continues to call individuals into His service, whether as full-time church workers or as volunteers. He likewise calls us to let go of earlier assignments and move into new areas of service. God knows our needs as His people, and He will provide for us and sustain us in fruitful service.

❖ **Gracious God, You provide pastors, teachers, and leaders to guide us in Your ways, calling them by grace. Give me a ready heart and steady hands. Amen.**

Today, we often think about God's grace in terms of what God has provided. This is good. However, we should also consider what God has prevented. God has prevented many calamities from striking us as part of His work of salvation for our lives.

❖ **Father, when the troubles of life do not make sense to us, strengthen us in faith through Christ. Amen.**

In a dream, God carries Ezekiel to a valley filled with dry bones and calls him to prophesy over them. Through Ezekiel's word, the dead receive life. The people receive hope of restoration. God's Word is effective and still has power to give new life and hope.

✤ **Almighty God, You alone speak the words of eternal life. Save us, Lord, for we cannot save ourselves. Amen.**

_____

_____

_____

_____

_____

_____

_____

_____

_____

_____

_____

_____

_____

_____

_____

_____

_____

_____

_____

_____

_____

_____

Ezekiel tours the temple and sees the exacting standards by which God measures man. Because God holds us to His standards, we find ourselves woefully inadequate. Yet, God graciously covers our inadequacies with Christ's blood and makes us partakers of His holiness.

✜ **Lord, have mercy on us. We are sinful and unclean. Wash us in the blood of the Lamb; make us wholly Yours. Amen.**

God instructs Ezekiel on the rebuilding of the altar and the sacrifices necessary to sanctify it so that God can again dwell with His people. Today, Christ's cross is your altar by which the Lord has consecrated you as His child.

❖ **Lord, keep me mindful of the sacrifice of Your dear Son for my salvation. Amen.**

_____

_____

_____

_____

_____

_____

_____

_____

_____

_____

_____

_____

_____

_____

_____

_____

_____

_____

_____

_____

God's Holy Law guides your relationship with Him and with others. Unfortunately, you cannot keep His Law rightly. Yet, Christ kept God's Laws perfectly in your stead and for your consecration.

❖ **Father, I daily sin much and do not deserve Your mercy. Grant me daily repentance and renew me through Christ, my Lord. Amen.**

The prince embodied Israel's role in worship, enacting roles of both a priest and a king, as David and Solomon had. What Ezekiel describes anticipates the coming of the greatest Son of David, your Lord Jesus Christ, who hallows your worship and presents your prayers to the heavenly Father.

✢ **Lord Jesus, watch over my worship, I earnestly pray. Feed me and nourish me with Your Holy Word. Amen.**

_____

_____

_____

_____

_____

_____

_____

_____

_____

_____

_____

_____

_____

_____

_____

_____

_____

_____

_____

_____

_____

_____

_____

_____

The idealized promised land is the prophetic symbol of a place in time in which the type of worship described previously will be possible. "The LORD Is There" (48:35) symbolizes what God has done for you through Jesus Christ. He has become your God. Through the forgiveness of sins, He dwells with you forever. God keeps His covenant!

❖   **Lord, You are faithful. Your mercy grants me eternal life through the blood of Christ Jesus, my Lord. Amen.**

Daniel and his friends determine not to violate God's laws, even though they live in a heathen environment. When you are tempted by worldly pressures to sin against the Lord, call to mind the example of these God-fearing youths. Your Lord, the Savior, is with you even now, and He will not forsake you.

❖ **Heavenly King, strengthen my resolve to follow Your Word. Amen.**

When life's mysteries or challenges threaten you, turn for guidance and comfort to the Lord and His Word. He knows all things and will hear your prayer. His Son, your Savior, intercedes for you.

✤ **Dear Jesus, may I never think of You as being distant or absent but always present for me in Your Word and Sacrament. Amen.**

Nebuchadnezzar builds a golden statue and at its dedication commands all people to worship it. Such worship is forbidden in the First Commandment (Exodus 20:3–6). Today, the gods we are tempted to worship may take subtler forms: material things, power, self. Only one "image" brings life and salvation—the incarnate Son of God (Colossians 1:15–20).

✤ **Triune God, may I never worship anyone or anything but You alone. Amen.**

_____

_____

_____

_____

_____

_____

_____

_____

_____

_____

_____

_____

_____

_____

_____

_____

_____

_____

_____

_____

_____

God, whom Belshazzar mocks, suddenly shows His presence. This is a warning for us all. "Do not be deceived: God is not mocked" (Galatians 6:7). God calls for repentance and faith. He likewise provides faithful interpreters of His Word to make His Law and promises known.

❖ **Holy God, may I ever respect Your almighty power and heed Your saving Word. Amen.**

DATE

TOPICS

Daniel 6:1–28

When Daniel is saved from the lions' den, Darius issues a new decree ordering all people in his kingdom to fear the God of Daniel. These events are a preview of God's ultimate triumph over all the forces of evil. The devil, that roaring lion (1 Peter 5:8), means deadly woe, but we tremble not (*LSB* 656)! For Christ is our protector.

✤ **All praise to You, O Christ, for conquering Satan and rescuing me from his deadly threats. Amen.**

In the vision of a ram and a male goat, God assures His people that His sanctuary will be restored. When trouble comes into our lives, no matter what its source, we may also ask, "How long?" Whether our time of suffering is long or short, we know that God hears our prayers and will help us according to His timetable.

❖ **Heavenly Father, comfort me with the assurance that Your love surrounds me every moment of my life. Amen.**

God demonstrates His love for Daniel by immediately responding to his prayer. Today, we have Jesus' assurance that He will hear and answer the prayers of His disciples (John 14:13–14; 15:16; 16:23–24). Therefore, we may pray with confidence and patience, knowing that God will hear.

❖ **Lord, hear my prayer and answer me as You know best. Grant me great patience and faith in Your love. Amen.**

_____

_____

_____

_____

_____

_____

_____

_____

_____

_____

_____

_____

_____

_____

_____

_____

_____

_____

_____

_____

_____

Believers have always been curious about when the end of the world is coming. Jesus made clear that no one knows that day and hour (Mark 13:32). The angel's advice to Daniel, to "go your way," is good for us all. Know that you are in God's hand, and take comfort that He has allotted a place in heaven for you.

❖ **Almighty Father, I wait for You to guide my life as I go on my way to my heavenly home. Amen.**

Wealth often begins to lead us into the same failings as those of Israel in Hosea's day, putting our trust in things rather than in the Lord. Fortunately for us, however, God's Law continues to show us our sins and to make us want to be rid of them. Through Christ, all our waywardness and idolatry is forgiven, and a new and all-inclusive covenant has been enacted.

❖ **O Lord, renew our relationship with You through the strength of Your faithfulness and commitment. Amen.**

It is a great comfort to know that the Church ultimately depends on Christ, the true Good Shepherd. The Resurrected One promises that He will never lose any of the sheep the Father has given Him but will keep them and raise them up on the Last Day.

❖ **Lord, preserve us from abuse and from abusing others. Amen.**

Even committed Christians manifest stubbornness and inability to overcome their weaknesses. The Lord continues to call us to repentance so that we might return to Him, confess our sin, trust in His pardoning love, and again be reminded that Jesus, the Lamb of God, has forgiven us.

✥ **Lord, have mercy on me, a sinner, and grant me peace. Amen.**

_____

_____

_____

_____

_____

_____

_____

_____

_____

_____

_____

_____

_____

_____

_____

_____

_____

_____

_____

_____

_____

Topping the list of Israel's misdeeds is idolatry. We, too, begin to fall into idolatry whenever we fear, love, and trust anything or any person more than the true God. Admitting that, we should also remember that the same God threatening to punish idolatry is also the One whose forgiving love and sustaining Spirit never fails.

❖   **Lord, help me to fear, love, and trust in You above all things. Amen.**

We need to hear warnings of judgment today, not only to prevent us from slipping into thanklessness, but also to check our inclinations toward willful sins and outright rebellion. The prophetic word we need to hear most, however, is that in Christ God has rained down righteousness upon us, forgiving all sin, and thus we have the very hope of glory.

❖   **O Lord, continually strengthen our conviction that on Judgment Day You will speak for us, not against us. Amen.**

_____

_____

_____

_____

_____

_____

_____

_____

_____

_____

_____

_____

_____

_____

_____

_____

_____

_____

_____

_____

Many today follow the lead of Hosea's generation, closing their ears to God's Law and imagining that judgment will never come upon them. Hear the Father's roar! Tremble and return by faith in Christ, who bore God's judgment for us and for our peace.

❖ **Heavenly Father, I believe. Help me in my weakness and unbelief, for the sake of Your only-begotten Son, my Savior. Amen.**

The children offered to Baal would be ripped away. Today, offer yourself, your family, and your congregation to the Lord in repentant prayer. Acknowledge lack of control and beg God's forgiveness, restoration, and health. He will ransom and redeem His people through His Son's compassionate love.

✣ **Jesus, may I always trust in You when faced with sin, death, and the power of the devil. Amen.**

_____

_____

_____

_____

_____

_____

_____

_____

_____

_____

_____

_____

_____

_____

_____

_____

_____

_____

_____

_____

_____

_____

The overwhelming evidence of Israel's apostasy showed that Hosea's indictment was true. In our own cases, the verdict is similarly clear. However, Jesus Christ has borne our sentence for us. The dew of His mercy and the shade of His cross heal our apostasy. He renders us innocent before God's holy tribunal.

❖ **Lord Jesus, enable us to walk in Your ways now and always. Amen.**

Desperation and starvation will result from the people's refusal to repent. Unchecked sins bring about disastrous consequences. However, remember that God often uses bad things to bring us to repentance and to accomplish His good and gracious will. The ultimate example of this is Christ's mournful death, which atoned for the sin of the world.

❖ **Whenever our hearts are tempted to turn away from You, O Lord, bring us back. Amen.**

_____

_____

_____

_____

_____

_____

_____

_____

_____

_____

_____

_____

_____

_____

_____

_____

_____

_____

_____

_____

_____

After the devastation wrought by the threatened locust plagues, the Lord promises to pour out His life-giving Spirit. Knowing that the Lord's judgment may come anytime, we should remain ever watchful and strive to be ready for that day. By His grace, the Lord enables us to do this very thing, as we call on Jesus' name and trust that He shall save us.

❖ **Heavenly Father, move us to trust in Your promised Redeemer, in whose name we will be saved. Amen.**

Joel announces that the Lord will punish His enemies, while vindicating and finally delivering His people. Though thoughts of judgment naturally produce dread in us, by faith we need not fear God's verdict. After all, the Lord is coming to usher us into heaven, not to punish us.

❖ **Lord, grant us full confidence for Judgment Day, for we believe that there is no longer any condemnation for those who are in Christ Jesus. Amen.**

Judah is guilty of listening to false prophets and worshiping in ways unbecoming the one true God. Sadly, we, too, are tempted and led astray by false theologies. However, it is the Lord's Word of Gospel alone that washes away our sin and bestows life for the sake of our Savior, Jesus Christ.

❖ **Gracious Lord, have mercy on Your people. Make our hearts swift to believe Your Word. Amen.**

Wealth, compromise of confession, and indifference to suffering tempt the "new Israel," the Church, still today. Recognizing such failures in ourselves should move us to repentance and increased gratitude for Christ, who was rich, yet became poor for our sakes, so that through His poverty we might become eternally rich (2 Corinthians 8:9).

❖   **Walk with us, O Lord. Abide with us, and restore us according to Your favor. Amen.**

_____

_____

_____

_____

_____

_____

_____

_____

_____

_____

_____

_____

_____

_____

_____

_____

_____

_____

_____

_____

_____

_____

God's first expectation has ever been and will always be "You shall have no other gods before Me" (Exodus 20:3). Amos teaches us that grace and faith are the true basis for worship and a right relationship to the Lord.

❖   **Lord, roll down justice and mercy upon us through the righteous sacrifice offered by Your Son for our forgiveness. Amen.**

People today imagine that their material prosperity is a sign that they need not humble themselves and turn away from complacency. However, God desires to give Himself to us. This is why His Son became incarnate for us and for our salvation.

✤ **Keep us, dear heavenly Father, from greed and sinful presumption upon Your grace. Amen.**

The people of Israel have now dared to openly despise the prophetic word even as it is being spoken to them. This scenario reminds us just how dangerous it is to ignore God's Word and to defy those sent to call us to repentance. Though guilty ourselves of similar failings, we take comfort in Christ's loyalty and unbounded forgiveness.

❖ **Lord, open our hearts and move our wills to hold Your Word sacred and gladly hear and learn it. Amen.**

If we persist in doing evil and despising God's graciousness, we will receive the same reward as the people of Israel—punishment from God and eternal separation from His life-giving Word. Treasure the Word! Our God is gracious and continually stands ready to receive the repentant heart and lift it up with His Word of forgiveness and peace in Jesus.

❖ **Lord, graciously receive my confession, and cover me with the forgiveness of Him who died and rose again. Amen.**

Amos's prophecy unexpectedly ends with a word of hope. A day of rich blessing is coming, for the Lord will fulfill His covenant promises, bring about restoration, and establish the eternal kingdom of His Messiah.

❖ **"Have mercy on me, O God, according to Your steadfast love; according to Your abundant mercy blot out my transgressions" (Psalm 51:1). Amen.**

God will judge nations and individuals according to their deeds, and all will come up short. However, God in Christ provided the righteousness needed to stand in His holy presence. All who believe His saving promise will receive refuge and deliverance from sin, death, and the devil.

❖ **Heavenly Father, strengthen my faith and lead me to show compassion, especially to those who need to hear the Gospel of forgiveness. Amen.**

_____

_____

_____

_____

_____

_____

_____

_____

_____

_____

_____

_____

_____

_____

_____

_____

_____

_____

_____

_____

_____

_____

_____

The apostle Paul, like Jonah, once felt that he had "received the sentence of death," but the God "who raises the dead" delivered him (2 Corinthians 1:8–10). All sinners deserve the sentence of everlasting death. But the God to whom salvation belongs has, in Christ, rescued us and given us new life.

❖   **Gracious God and Father, thank You for redeeming me from sin, death, and the power of the devil. Amen.**

Jonah has a precious opportunity to preach God's Word to Nineveh, but his heart is not in it. May we never be found guilty of neglecting our mission to make disciples of all nations. Praise God, He did not neglect us but appointed His only-begotten Son as our Savior.

❖ **O Lord, reveal to me every opportunity I have to share the good news of salvation with others, no matter who they are. Amen.**

_____

_____

_____

_____

_____

_____

_____

_____

_____

_____

_____

_____

_____

_____

_____

_____

_____

_____

_____

_____

_____

In mercy, God promises to gather a remnant out of Israel and shepherd them. Today, the Lord calls us to help our neighbors protect their house and possessions in fear and love. Jesus is our Good Shepherd, who gave His life to redeem us from sin and everlasting death. He has satisfied our most pressing needs and will free us from covetous desires.

✤ **Lord Jesus, my Good Shepherd, guide my feet in the way of Your Commandments. Amen.**

When we face difficult times, when the forces of the devil are lined up against us, we may be tempted to give up trusting that God is with us to guide and protect us. We can be certain of His gracious presence whenever we hear His Word and receive the body and blood of Christ. He will not leave us or forsake us.

❖ **Father, thank You for giving me Your Son, in whom I have life and security and peace. Amen.**

When we take the Lord at His Word and depend on His might, we will be secure and at peace. God remains present with us even when we feel utterly abandoned to forces beyond our control, such as sickness and death. He uses such times to cleanse us from unbelief and lead us to a deeper trust in Christ Jesus.

❖ **Thank You, Father, for always being with me no matter where I find myself in life. Amen.**

Whoever breaks God's laws, especially by using positions of power to exploit the weak, will ultimately face God's judgment. Our sins may not match all that the Lord here condemns, but none of us is innocent in His sight. To walk humbly with our God means to repent daily of our sins and cling to His grace and mercy in Christ.

❖   **Lord Jesus, cleanse me from all evil, and give me strength to care for those who are weak and powerless in our world. Amen.**

The Lord's loving and forgiving nature is described, followed by a confident assertion of faith in Him. To know and trust such a God provokes in us a humble awe of our own unworthiness. With the tax collector in the temple, we are moved to pray, "God, be merciful to me, a sinner!" (Luke 18:13).

✤   **I hope in You, O Lord. Never leave me or forsake me. Amen.**

Nahum mockingly describes the sudden, devastating siege and capture
of Nineveh, the city once known for its ruthlessness and cruelty. God
will not leave unpunished those whose way of life is violence and force
(cf. Matthew 26:52). God has revealed a different way, one of mercy and
peace through His Son, the Prince of Peace.

✣   **Lord, guide our feet into the way of peace. Amen.**

_____

_____

_____

_____

_____

_____

_____

_____

_____

_____

_____

_____

_____

_____

_____

_____

_____

_____

_____

_____

Human beings dare never sit in judgment of God's ways, which are beyond human discernment (Romans 9:20; 11:33). We, however, can place our trust in Him, confident that in the end He will carry out His beneficial will in our lives.

❖ **Help me to submit to You, O Lord, and trust in Your mercy. Amen.**

_____

_____

_____

_____

_____

_____

_____

_____

_____

_____

_____

_____

_____

_____

_____

_____

_____

_____

_____

The Book that begins with a complaint now ends with an expression of joyful confidence in the God of salvation. When we look to ourselves and our own strength, we have reason only to despair. But when we are cast down and experience inner turmoil, we say, "Yet I will rejoice in the Lord; I will take joy in the God of my salvation" (v. 18).

✤   **I will praise You for Your salvation, O Lord, all the days of my life. Amen.**

_____

_____

_____

_____

_____

_____

_____

_____

_____

_____

_____

_____

_____

_____

_____

_____

_____

_____

_____

_____

_____

Zephaniah urges the people of Judah to seek the Lord, then describes the devastation that will fall on neighboring nations because of their sins. We, too, are guilty of arrogance, pride, and boasting. The Lord calls us to humble repentance and, through trust in Jesus as our Savior, He promises to shield us from His anger.

❖   **Lord, may I never boast except in the cross of Jesus, my Savior. Amen.**

Zephaniah urges God's people to rejoice over their coming salvation. Fear may hinder us from witnessing of God's love and mercy; how wrong and foolish that would be! God has redeemed us in Christ. He will always be with us, and someday He will take us to the heavenly Jerusalem.

❖ **Lord God, make me a bold witness of Your saving power. Amen.**

Do we at times become discouraged thinking that God's Church and the preaching of His Word count for nothing in this world? The Lord assures us that it is here we find our greatest treasure: forgiveness of sins and peace in Christ our Savior.

✤   **Praise to You, O Lord, for establishing Your glorious Church and for the peace that she proclaims. Amen.**

At a moment when God seems remote and uncaring, Zechariah sees that He is guiding events for good. If you experience dismal moments, do not succumb to the despairing thought that God has forsaken His people in general or you in particular. God's angels watch over His own, and Christ effectually intercedes for you before His Father's throne.

❖ **Lord, give me courage and endurance to trust that if Christ is for me, the hosts of hell cannot prevail against me. Amen.**

We are all like brands plucked from the fire of sin; we all wear filthy garments. But because of Christ, the greater Joshua, we have been robed in righteousness. We enjoy the peace and safety of His kingdom.

❖ **Holy God, give me eyes to see and confess my filthiness and a heart to believe Your perfect cleansing, through Jesus Christ, my Lord. Amen.**

God uses earthly leaders to build His kingdom of believers, the communion of saints. Yet no pastor, teacher, or layperson can keep the lamp of faith and holy living alight by his or her own efforts. The Holy Spirit gives life and strength to believers through Word and Sacrament to build God's holy temple of living stones (1 Peter 2:5).

❖   Holy Spirit, make me strong in faith so that I may better serve as one of Your instruments. Amen.

_____

_____

_____

_____

_____

_____

_____

_____

_____

_____

_____

_____

_____

_____

_____

_____

_____

_____

_____

_____

God's curse rests on all who fail to keep His Law perfectly (Galatians 3:10), but in Christ, that curse is removed. For "Christ redeemed us from the curse of the law by becoming a curse for us" (Galatians 3:13). How blessed we are that our debt was canceled by having it nailed to the cross!

✤   **Lord Jesus Christ, thank You for removing God's curse, which rested on me because of my sin. Assist me as I share this Good News with others. Amen.**

The Lord's authority is likened to strong horses pulling four chariots, patrolling the earth in all directions. This is also our God, powerful and active in controlling the events of this world for the sake of His people and for the sake of the Gospel. God's word to us is that He is our refuge and strength (cf. Psalm 46:1).

✣   **Almighty Father, Creator and Ruler of all that exists, silence our doubts and fears by Your comforting Word. Amen.**

_____

_____

_____

_____

_____

_____

_____

_____

_____

_____

_____

_____

_____

_____

_____

_____

_____

_____

_____

_____

In Zechariah's day, priest and people alike needed to learn the lessons from Judah's history lest the errors that caused such distress be repeated. God also wants us to examine our actions and ask whether the things we do glorify Him. In Christ alone is complete cleansing from all iniquity.

✤ **Lord of hosts, may Your Word ever be "a lamp to my feet and a light to my path" (Psalm 119:105). Amen.**

God was good to Israel, and He has been good to us. We do not deserve His goodness, for there is no merit or worthiness in us. Yet His grace has allowed us to see in Christ the spiritual fulfillment of many of His ancient promises. As people who trust in His mercy, we look forward to a glorious future and seek to serve Him in all we say and do.

❖   **Lord, give me a thankful heart, and move me to glorify You in word and deed. Amen.**

_____

_____

_____

_____

_____

_____

_____

_____

_____

_____

_____

_____

_____

_____

_____

_____

_____

_____

_____

_____

_____

_____

God's enemies suffer defeat for breaking His Holy Law. They will learn that "the wages of sin is death" (Romans 6:23). But those who repent and cling in faith to the Messiah will be covered with His righteousness and enjoy His rule of peace.

✣ **King Jesus, accept my joyful shouts of praise for Your saving work. Rule in my life, now and always. Amen.**

When confronted by spiritual foes who cause us to feel weak and helpless, we must keep telling ourselves that our strength is in the One "who stretched out the heavens and founded the earth" (12:1). He will protect and save us.

❖ **Lord, my refuge and strength, remove all fear from my heart, and make me confident of Your ultimate victory. Amen.**

Throughout history, false religion has been a serious problem. People today may not call on Baal or Rimmon for help, but idols and false prophets are still in evidence. Idols may be gone from our eyes but not from our hearts. Only when Christ comes again in glory will there be an end to all false religion.

❖ **Lord, keep me steadfast in Your Word, safe from all who would deceive me. Amen.**

John and Zechariah both foresee a day when the Lord will use His mighty power to crush all His enemies and make all things new and holy. Those wearing white robes, whose sins have been washed away in the blood of the Lamb, will reside in that Holy City (Revelation 7:13–14).

❖ **"Now come, Thou Blessed One, Lord Jesus, God's own Son, Hail! Hosanna! We enter all The wedding hall To eat the Supper at Thy call." Amen.** (*LSB* 516:2)

_____

_____

_____

_____

_____

_____

_____

_____

_____

_____

_____

_____

_____

_____

_____

_____

_____

_____

_____

The people in Malachi's day ask, "Where is the God of justice?" (cf. 2 Peter 3:4). The Lord makes it very clear that the Day of Judgment is coming. He wants all people to be prepared for that day. That's why He sent the Messenger of the new covenant, Jesus Christ, to suffer and die for the sins of the world.

❖ **Blessed Lord and Savior, help me to wait and pray for Your reappearing with confidence and hope. Amen.**

Malachi concludes with the Lord's announcement that Judgment Day is coming. For those who refuse to repent and believe the Gospel, it means utter destruction. But for those who fear His name, this will be a day of rejoicing. John the Baptist called the people of his day to repentance and faith in the coming Savior. How great a message for us to hear!

❖ **Dear Lord Jesus, let the light of Your healing grace shine on me, that I may fear, love, and trust in You always. Amen.**

The events of his life may have seemed confusing to Joseph, but God had a plan. All of the Lord's leading was to fulfill Old Testament prophecies. We do not always know where God is leading us, but we can be sure that He will be with us and that His plans are for our good.

✤ **Loving Father, help me to pray with Jesus, "Your will be done," and follow where You lead. Amen.**

DATE

TOPICS

Matthew 3:1–4:25

The devil tempts Jesus to seek His own glory. Jesus refuses this path to walk the way of the cross. In love, He did all this for our sake, because we have failed God's test. Jesus is our substitute who defeated Satan for us, setting us free from sin, death, and the devil's power.

✤ **Mighty Hero, though devils fill the world, we do not fear because You have won the victory. Amen.**

_____

_____

_____

_____

_____

_____

_____

_____

_____

_____

_____

_____

_____

_____

_____

_____

_____

_____

_____

_____

_____

Jesus' teachings in the Sermon on the Mount show us our sins and describe the path on which we, as repentant children of God, seek to walk. Our Lord and Savior declares us blessed and calls us to be lights of the world because we are enlightened by His Word.

❖ **Dear Jesus, walk with me on the narrow way that leads to life, lest I stumble or stray. Amen.**

In the Sermon on the Mount, Jesus had demonstrated His teaching authority (7:29). Jesus uses that same divine authority in working miracles. His miracles are signs that anticipate the day when every disease and even death itself will be no more (Revelation 21:4). Then, as forgiven sinners, we will rejoice with all those who have been cleansed.

❖   **Precious Savior, fill me with anticipation for that day when You will heal every illness. Amen.**

People commonly experience disappointment because of false or unfulfilled expectations. We hope God will act in a certain way, but He does not. We then wonder why. To guard against false expectations, focus on Jesus and on what He has said and done. He is the fulfillment of all our hopes.

❖   **Lord Jesus, remind me of Your words and works that assure me of Your saving love. Amen.**

Just as the people of Nazareth took offense at Jesus and refused to believe in Him, so today many are skeptical of His claims. If we hear and understand, it is not by our own reason or strength but because the Holy Spirit has created faith in our hearts by the Gospel. Only the Spirit, working through the Word, can change an unbeliever's heart.

❖   **Spirit of God, thank You for calling me by the Gospel and enlightening my heart. Amen.**

_____

_____

_____

_____

_____

_____

_____

_____

_____

_____

_____

_____

_____

_____

_____

_____

_____

_____

_____

_____

_____

The two great feeding miracles of Jesus remind us of how God miraculously fed His people Israel with manna and quail in the wilderness (Exodus 16; Numbers 11). God works through His creation to provide our daily bread. We dare not take this blessing for granted.

❖　**Heavenly Father, thank You for abundantly answering my prayer: "Give us this day our daily bread." Amen.**

Peter's confession of Jesus as the Messiah and Son of God was a key event in Jesus' ministry. To confess Jesus as Savior and Lord is also essential in every believer's life. Like Peter, none of us can by our own reason or strength believe in Jesus Christ. The Holy Spirit has called us by the Gospel.

❖ **Grant us grace, heavenly Father, to confess Jesus and so remain on the unshakable rock of our salvation. Amen.**

We cannot earn eternal life through our good works; we can only receive it by God's grace. But Jesus still rewards our sacrifices and service for Him. Through faith in Christ, God freely gives us the gift of eternal life. And if that were not enough, He rewards the sacrifices made for His kingdom a hundredfold!

❖   **Thank You, Father, for adopting us and making us heirs of eternal life. Amen.**

Like the crowds in Jerusalem, we are prone to fickleness—today all for the Lord, tomorrow turning from Him. Though we often prove faithless, Jesus remains constant. His love and forgiveness never falter.

❖　**Heavenly Father, keep us united by faith to Christ, our source of life, lest we ever turn away, reject Him, and so lose our hope of salvation. Amen.**

Jesus laments the fact that so many of His people reject Him and the gift of eternal life. Even when hated and rejected by many, Jesus never stopped loving and sincerely reaching out to them. He does the same with us.

✣ **Fill us with Your unbounded love, O Lord, that we never cease to love and long for the salvation of all, even for those who revile You and hate us as Your disciples. Amen.**

On the Last Day, Jesus will separate true believers from hypocrites and those who reject Him. The faithful will be vindicated and welcomed into heaven, while unbelievers will be condemned. Having received forgiveness through faith in Christ, God's flock eagerly await the day on which they shall be publicly vindicated and receive eternal life.

✤ **Grant us a faith that perseveres until the end, O Lord. Amen.**

Jesus is crucified and reviled on every hand. Here we see the full depth of our sin: the pain of the cross and the reviling of the whole world is what we deserve. But we also see the full depth of God's mercy in that He willingly submitted Himself to this torture for our sakes.

✣ **Grant, O God, that I boast in nothing but in the cross of Your Son. Amen.**

Christ commissions His disciples to go and make disciples of all nations through Baptism and teaching. Today, remember your Baptism and confirmation in the faith, which are precious blessings for the Lord's disciples. His love and care are new for you every morning.

✤ **Send us, Lord, to make disciples in Your name in accordance with our callings in life. Amen.**

_____

_____

_____

_____

_____

_____

_____

_____

_____

_____

_____

_____

_____

_____

_____

_____

_____

_____

_____

_____

The invitation to discipleship confronts people today: either drop everything and, in faith, follow Jesus and make sacrifices, or run the risk of missing out on the Kingdom. Thankfully, we are not left to our own devices in this regard. God's Holy Spirit, working through the Word and Sacraments, moves us to faithful discipleship and so also to eternal life.

❖ **Lord, thank You for calling us into Your kingdom, for which You declare us fit by Your grace. Amen.**

Precisely because the Kingdom grows so slowly and its Lord is so patient, believers tend to become discouraged and its enemies are emboldened. But in the end, the Kingdom alone will stand, and everything else will be overthrown.

❖ **Lord, let us see both in fact and by faith that Your kingdom will someday be all in all. Keep us ever sheltered safely within its branches. Amen.**

When problems threaten us and needs overwhelm our resources, what is our reaction? Do we turn first to the Lord? We should, as His Word makes clear, for He still treats His flock with compassion and more than provides for every need of body and soul.

✤ **Lord, thank You for providing so abundantly and for graciously sustaining our bodies and souls. Teach us to turn to You first in every want and need. Amen.**

Jesus warns that He has come to suffer, die, and rise and that everyone who follows Him must carry the cross. Temptation to avoid the anguish of the cross is great. A safe life tempts us to deny Christ and His cross. Yet, Jesus suffered for our salvation and promised to overcome Satan and all our foes. Jesus is the only one sufficient to exchange His life for ours.

❖ **Lord, strengthen us to follow You from Your cross to Your glory. Amen.**

Confused by Jesus' prediction of His death, the disciples return to a subject they know well, their own greatness. When we are tempted to debate who is the greatest, we should instead look to where the Master hangs on the cross. He represents us before the Father in order to redeem us, and He leads us by the cross into a new life.

❖   **Lord, remind us that You alone are great, for You have served the least among us. Amen.**

Salvation is a gift of grace through faith in Jesus Christ. We do not earn God's love and favor by keeping the Law, especially when we look for loopholes to excuse our sinful behavior (cf. 10:1–12). All people, like helpless children, receive Jesus' blessing and enter the Kingdom through faith in Him.

❖ **Dear Father, lead us to give ourselves for others, that we, being last, might truly be first with Jesus in His kingdom. Amen.**

_____

_____

_____

_____

_____

_____

_____

_____

_____

_____

_____

_____

_____

_____

_____

_____

_____

_____

_____

_____

_____

Opponents of Jesus confront Him and question His authority. Jesus refuses to engage them since He confidently knows the true character of His authority (Matthew 28:18). The anger of these leaders brings Jesus ever nearer to the cross, where He acts in weakness to overthrow the authority of the evil one for the sake of our salvation.

✦   **Lord God, cleanse the hearts of Your people, that they may be temples for Your Holy Spirit. Amen.**

As Christians proclaim Law and Gospel, they need to be ready to endure the loss of everything, including their lives. Because God wants all people to hear the Gospel, He prolongs the New Testament age so that the Church may witness to all the earth.

✤　"Lord of harvest, great and kind, Rouse to action heart and mind; Let the gath'ring nations all See Your light and heed Your call." Amen. (*LSB* 830:6)

Jesus fulfills the Scripture that promises the forgiveness of sins through the sacrifice of the Shepherd, even though all His sheep desert Him. Good intentions do not substitute for faith. Only through God's strength can any Christian face trial. Even though Jesus' sheep will run away, He will lay down His life for them.

✤ **Faithful Shepherd, keep me close this day and always. Amen.**

Jesus is crucified, bearing the punishment for the sins of the world. This is what it costs to atone for sins. At any time, Jesus can halt the proceedings, save Himself, and condemn His enemies. His love for us and His obedience to the Father lead Him to make this sacrifice instead.

❖ **Dearest Jesus, give me boldness to confess You before the world. Amen.**

_____

_____

_____

_____

_____

_____

_____

_____

_____

_____

_____

_____

_____

_____

_____

_____

_____

_____

Jesus commissions His followers to proclaim the message of salvation throughout the world. Only through faith in Jesus Christ can anyone be saved. The Gospel invitation is open to all. God wants all people to be saved through Jesus (1 Timothy 2:3–4).

❖   **"Christ is arisen From the grave's dark prison. So let our joy rise full and free; Christ our comfort true will be. Alleluia!" Amen.** (*LSB* 459:1)

God faithfully keeps His promises by sending one like Elijah to prepare His people, and then by announcing the advent of the Son of God and Savior of all humankind. Nothing is impossible with God! Through Jesus' life, death, and resurrection, we are bold to hope for an even more wonderful fulfillment of divine promises, including our glorification.

❖   **Blessed are You, O Lord, for You have visited and redeemed Your people and raised up a horn of salvation for us. Amen.**

_____

Luke's account of John's ministry and Jesus' ancestry hint at the universal nature of the Messiah's kingdom. How sad, then, that churches too often show little concern for those outside the immediate boundaries of their fellowship. The Gospel is for everyone! Jesus' death and resurrection bring life and salvation to all who repent and call on His name.

❖ **Lord, move me to reach out with the Good News that leads to everlasting life. Amen.**

A miraculous catch of fish shows the disciples that Jesus is more than a great teacher—God is working mightily through Him. Like the disciples, the mundane struggle for daily bread, and the sin and doubt it fosters, may make you feel distant from God. But He is ever near and also ever prepared to forgive your sins.

❖   **Stay with me, Lord, for I am a sinful person. Grant me repentance and a new life in service to You. Amen.**

Jesus continues to call people for various roles of service in the Church, depending on God's order, our gifts, and the Church's needs. There are no self-appointed offices in God's Church. He calls people and extends His care by His gracious and good will.

❖   **Lord Jesus, lead me to know the blessings of a life that reflects Your divine qualities of compassion, forbearance, and forgiveness. Amen.**

After displaying His mastery over nature and demons, Jesus shows His authority over incurable illness and even death. Just as the disciples despaired in the face of danger (8:25), we also sometimes despair as catastrophe looms. But Jesus can deal with any problem. His sacrificial death and victorious resurrection prove that He can overcome even the gravest threat.

✣   **Draw us ever to Your light, O Lord. Amen.**

Because Jesus is the only way to eternal life, following Him demands that we reorder our priorities, putting Him in first place and setting aside whatever does not accord with His way. This proves impossible for us but not for our Lord, who embraces and bears our crosses and shame that He might present us righteous before His dear Father.

❖　**O Lord, grant me humility, that I might please You in all that I do and say. Amen.**

In contrast with Jesus' demand for great works in the previous parable (vv. 25–37), the story of Mary and Martha shows the importance of faith and rest in Jesus and His Word. Today, we are often so distracted that we neglect what matters most: God's Word and Sacraments.

✣ **O Savior, bear my anxieties and remove my distractions, that I may receive Your good portion for me. Amen.**

_____

_____

_____

_____

_____

_____

_____

_____

_____

_____

_____

_____

_____

_____

_____

_____

_____

_____

_____

_____

_____

_____

Measure all traditions against God's Word, especially the standards of mercy Jesus emphasized. Give thanks to God for faithful traditions that agree with His Gospel, which alone grants us salvation in Christ.

✜   **Lord Jesus, when earthly relations cause me to make You and Your kingdom anything less than my first priority, strengthen me and lead me back into the way of life everlasting. Amen.**

Jesus points out tragedies as occasions for self-examination and reflection on our sinful frailty. Contrary to popular thought, tragedy does not always strike people because they somehow deserve it. Rather, in His wisdom God allows and uses even tragic events to warn of judgment, that He might bring us to repentance and eternal life through faith in Jesus.

✤ **Lord, grant me humility before those mysteries that surpass my understanding. Amen.**

_____

_____

_____

_____

_____

_____

_____

_____

_____

_____

_____

_____

_____

_____

_____

_____

_____

_____

_____

_____

_____

_____

Jesus illustrates how pride leads to humiliation. Let others praise you or promote you rather than praise and promote yourself. No matter what others say or do, your greatest promotion is when the heavenly Father calls you His beloved child, through Christ.

✤ **Grant me a humble and steadfast heart, O Lord, to see myself as You see me. Amen.**

In the first of three similar parables, Jesus uses the devotion of a shepherd to illustrate God's willingness to find the wayward sinner. God does not abandon us to our foolishness but seeks us out, calling us to repentance and to faith in the Gospel.

❖ **Bring us home, dear Lord, and let there be joy in heaven. Grant us daily repentance. Amen.**

The Pharisee excludes himself from God's gift of righteousness, while the penitent tax collector embraces it. Today, beware of the complacency of measuring your goodness against others. Measure yourself against God's standards—then repent. God is ready to justify the worst of sinners by His generous grace in Christ.

❖ **God, be merciful to me, a sinner. Amen.**

DATE

TOPICS

Jesus warns His disciples not to be impressed by the scribes' display. Do not practice the faith simply to impress others. In contrast, for your salvation, Jesus "made Himself nothing, taking the form of a servant. . . . He humbled Himself" (Philippians 2:7–8).

✣ **Lord, grant me the humility and mind of Christ. Amen.**

Jesus, before the Council, points to His exaltation. He acknowledges that He is the Son of God and is condemned. We can never force Jesus into our definitions of Messiah. It is for us to receive Him for who He is, as described in Scripture. Jesus, condemned for us, is the promised Messiah and Son of God, who now is seated in glory at God's right hand.

❖ **Jesus, You are the Christ, Son of God in glory. Grant that this confession may always be ours. Amen.**

Jesus includes the mission to all nations through the Holy Spirit's power. There is the danger that we keep to ourselves when Jesus is equipping us to go out—we accept the fact that He is risen but deny the mission on which He sends us. The resurrected Christ truly equips us for our witness to Him with the Holy Spirit, whom He provides.

❖ **Come, Holy Spirit, as promised by Jesus. Enable us to bear witness to our crucified and risen Savior. Amen.**

In Jerusalem, many come to believe in Jesus, but theirs is a superficial faith based mainly on the miracles they see. The all-knowing Christ calls us to abandon all outward pretense, to repent truly, and to trust Him fully. The Lord Jesus offers Himself in mercy and forgiveness to those who trust in Him.

❖ **O all-knowing Savior, forgive my secret sins and cover them with Your boundless love. Amen.**

John the Baptist steps aside when Christ comes because Jesus is the Son of God from heaven and possesses the Holy Spirit without measure. God reveals His wrath against those who do not believe in His Son and deprives them of everlasting life. But He gives everlasting life to all who trust in Jesus.

✦ **Jesus, give to me a full measure of Your Spirit, that I may always remain faithful to You and bear witness to You. Amen.**

_____

_____

_____

_____

_____

_____

_____

_____

_____

_____

_____

_____

_____

_____

_____

_____

_____

_____

_____

_____

_____

_____

Many today will not believe God's Word unless they are first shown demonstrative proofs. Despite such unbelief, the Lord Jesus hastens to call all people to faith; He would forgive them and bear their burdens and needs.

✜   **Lord Jesus, give me and my entire family unquestioning faith in Your promises. Amen.**

By walking on the storm-tossed sea, Jesus shows His disciples that He is the eternal King, ruler of all creation. Today, when life's problems overwhelm us, fear may cause us to lose faith in God's protection and care. But Jesus is true God and true man in one person; Jesus has saved us from sin and evil, assuring us of His divine protection in every situation.

❖ **Lighten our darkness, O Lord, and protect us against the dangers of the night. Amen.**

_____

_____

_____

_____

_____

_____

_____

_____

_____

_____

_____

_____

_____

_____

_____

_____

_____

_____

_____

_____

_____

_____

Jewish leaders and the populace hold sharply different opinions regarding Jesus. Today, people continue to misjudge the Lord on the basis of their own feelings and perceptions. Truly, "no one ever spoke like this man" Jesus; His teaching exceeded all human expectations, imparting grace to those who heard. His words came directly from our heavenly Father.

❖ **Lead me, Lord Jesus, to hear the full message of Your Word. Amen.**

Sheep who ignore the Good Shepherd's voice (His Word) have only themselves to blame and will fall prey to Satan. Unlike human love motivated by self-interest, Christ's love for His own moved Him to voluntarily endure even death on a cross for our sake (Philippians 2:8).

❖   **My dear Shepherd, watch over me that I may never stray from You. Amen.**

As Jesus concludes His public ministry, He reminds His hearers that He has come to save the world. Rejection of Christ and His Word brings judgment. Believers, however, do not see in Jesus an angry judge but a loving Savior who has our salvation ever on His heart.

❖ **Gracious Savior, remove from my heart all unbelief and doubt. Amen.**

Jesus washes His disciples' feet, thereby showing His willingness to serve them. Often we think that greatness means having others serve us. But Christ shows His true greatness and His love toward us in that He came to wash away our sins, even though it cost Him His life.

❖ **Lord Jesus Christ, receive our thanks for Your love, and help us to love one another as deeply as You have loved us. Amen.**

_____

_____

_____

_____

_____

_____

_____

_____

_____

_____

_____

_____

_____

_____

_____

_____

_____

_____

_____

_____

_____

_____

Christ predicts that His disciples will face hostility from the unbelieving world. Those who think it is easy to be a Christian fail to understand the real consequences of following Jesus Christ. In the face of persecution and the world's hatred, Christ promises to strengthen and keep us from falling away.

❖　**O Lord, let me not be discouraged when I am personally abused because of my faith. Amen.**

Knowing that He is going to the cross, Jesus prays for His disciples and asks that they be united by faith in Him. Whenever Christians ignore God's Word, they foster divisions within the Church and diminish their witness. But God's Word is the truth that will unite His Church, glorify Him, and enable His people to fulfill their calling in a troubled world.

❖ **Heavenly Father, reveal in my life the love that You have shown me in Your Son. Amen.**

John invites us to look on Jesus, the crucified "Lamb of God, who takes away the sin of the world" (1:29). Enemies of the cross interpret Jesus' death as disgrace, not glory. Yet, hidden beneath the outward "mask" of Jesus' suffering and death, there stands the work of our redemption, foretold in the Old Testament.

✣   **Through the witness of Your blessed apostles, Lord Jesus, draw many to Your saving grace. Amen.**

In the closing exchange between Jesus and Peter, Jesus kindly reminds this beloved apostle that God is in control of matters related to his future. All Christians must humbly recognize that God has not chosen to reveal certain things to us. But the Scriptures do reveal what is necessary for us to know: Jesus and the salvation He brings.

❖ **Blessed Lord, may we embrace and ever hold fast the glorious hope of everlasting life. Amen.**

_____

_____

_____

_____

_____

_____

_____

_____

_____

_____

_____

_____

_____

_____

_____

_____

_____

_____

_____

_____

_____

The disciples and others seek the Lord's will concerning the candidate of His choice to replace Judas as a leader of the Church, the new Israel. Today, entrust your future to the Lord in prayer. He will prepare your way before you. Since our Lord is present with us till the end of the age, He will knit together in love His faithful people with Himself and with one another.

❖ **Jesus, our King, may we never tire of watching in prayer before Your throne, and may Your will be our delight. Amen.**

The early Christians lived only for their Lord and for the other members of His Body, the Church. How cheap in comparison is our indifference to the Church. Yet the Holy Spirit still dwells and works among us; we still have the apostles' teaching embodied in the New Testament. How blessed are we in such heavenly fellowship!

✤   **Lord, open our eyes to Your reality, order our priorities, and let Your light transfigure these latter days. Amen.**

Peter shows the crowd at the temple that all the prophets have pointed to Jesus as the Christ. The risen Lord brings to light our hidden guilt and lifts the burden that crushes every sinner. Though His Word points out your shame, His grace will wipe away your sin.

✛   **Lord Jesus, come boldly to both Jew and Gentile, to accuse and to forgive, to wound and to heal. Amen.**

God heals many people through the apostles. This massive outpouring of God's love and power comes with His serious appeals for repentance. God's power to change lives is still at work today. His greatest work always remains the forgiveness of sins.

✤ **Lord, fill us with all due reverence for You and Your mysteries. Stretch forth Your hand to heal the sicknesses of our bodies and souls. Amen.**

God and His grace cannot be bought. A person's life is transformed only by the power of the Holy Spirit working through the Word. Today, ask the Lord to bless your study of His Word. He will transform you and bless your service according to His gifts and good pleasure.

✢   **Father, forgive me, for Jesus' sake, and let Your Holy Spirit work mightily in my life, that I might imitate Philip and proclaim Your Word of life. Amen.**

The Holy Spirit opened Saul's eyes and heart to forgiveness through Christ so he boldly confessed His name to his fellow Jews. Today, trust that the Lord is able to change people's lives—even people you regard as utterly lost and despicable. How great is our Lord and His grace!

❖   **Father, as Your Holy Spirit opened Saul's heart to the Gospel, open my heart, that I might believe and make a fearless testimony of Christ. Amen.**

Through the Law, God condemns all sinners and drives them to repentance; through the Gospel, He grants life everlasting. Live a life of daily repentance, and glorify God for His lavish blessings and gifts to you and all people.

❖ **Lord, let our likeness to some not be a barrier to others. Draw everyone to You, O Holy Spirit, even the unlikely. Amen.**

The death of James at the hand of Herod and the imprisonment of Peter demonstrate the world's hatred of the Gospel. Yet, nothing can separate believers from the love of Christ. He fulfills His purpose for us in life and in death; therefore, we have joy.

❖ **Father, may Rhoda's joy at seeing Peter overflow in my life as I have fellowship with other believers. Amen.**

Today, the unbelieving world often responds in opposition to the message of salvation. Yet, the Gospel of Christ's death and resurrection, which fulfilled the Old Testament promises of salvation, "is the power of God for salvation to everyone who believes" (Romans 1:16).

❖   **Heavenly Father, help me to realize that all of Your promises and actions are fulfilled in Jesus Christ to give me eternal life. Amen.**

The Jerusalem Council resolved the critical issue of who God's chosen people are and affirmed that Jews and Gentiles are saved by grace alone (v. 11). Obedience to the Law is a burden or yoke no one can bear, neither Jew nor Gentile (v. 10; cf. 13:39). However, our salvation through faith alone also empowers us to live with care and respect for others.

❖ **Heavenly Father, I praise You for saving us through the grace of our Lord Jesus. Amen.**

_____

_____

_____

_____

_____

_____

_____

_____

_____

_____

_____

_____

_____

_____

_____

_____

_____

_____

_____

_____

God guided Paul and his companions in unexpected directions. Our plans in general, and in particular our plans for the spread of the Gospel, do not always proceed as we hope. Yet, God directs us as His messengers to the people and places He would have us go. His grace is not bounded by our weakness but serves His good purposes in Christ.

❖ **Heavenly Father, continue to send workers into Your harvest field. Amen.**

These travels conclude Paul's second missionary journey and begin his third. Travel plans and visits may not always turn out the way you intend. When you travel, begin with prayer, and serve the Lord with purpose. Place your life in God's hands; He works all things according to His good and gracious will.

❖ **Lord, watch over me through Your guardian angels and strengthen me by the presence of my fellow believers. Amen.**

_____

_____

_____

_____

_____

_____

_____

_____

_____

_____

_____

_____

_____

_____

_____

_____

_____

_____

_____

_____

_____

_____

_____

_____

_____

Paul arrives at Ephesus and begins a very productive period of his ministry. Apart from Christ, there is no salvation. The Word of God clearly shows that Jesus Christ is the fulfillment of God's promises of eternal salvation for all. Through Holy Baptism, He consecrates us as His beloved people.

❖ **Lord Jesus, help us always to believe in You for eternal life. Help us also to share Your Good News. Amen.**

At times, you may be in situations where you are afraid to share openly your Christian beliefs. The crucified and risen Christ forgives you for any past failures to confess Him before others, yet He also promises to always be at your side and support your testimony (Matthew 28:20).

✛   **Jesus, You are the resurrection and the life. Make me bold, like Paul, so that I am never ashamed to speak Your truth. Amen.**

_____

_____

_____

_____

_____

_____

_____

_____

_____

_____

_____

_____

_____

_____

_____

_____

_____

_____

_____

_____

Paul makes his defense before King Agrippa. He describes his zealous opposition to Jesus and the Gospel message. Because we are born in sin (Psalm 51:5), we all have an ungodly past, even if we have never persecuted Christians the way Paul did. Be assured that Christ forgives and delivers us, just as He did Paul.

✢   **Jesus, let me see others with the love You have for them, and empower me to share the Gospel with them. Amen.**

Have you ever blamed God for the problems in your life? Have you forgotten that even through hardships, God is working for your benefit (Romans 8:28)? Rejoice today that His love and care for you are infinite (Romans 8:38–39)!

❖ **Lord, put all the problems in my life to good use. I praise You that nothing compares to the grace and mercy You show me, now and forever. Amen.**

We love to condemn the sins of others. We might not have committed some of the acts Paul condemns here, but we all have sinned. We have exchanged God's truth for human foolishness. Seeing sin, we ought not respond defensively but in confession. We know God's response to sin: He sent His Son to die for sinners.

❖ **Lord have mercy on me, a sinner. Grant me sincere confession and compassion for other sinners. Amen.**

Abraham trusted that God was able to do what He promised. Trials and challenges may tempt us to doubt God's promises. As He did with Abraham, God will strengthen our faith, assure us of His promises, help us to trust, and fulfill all He said He would do.

❖ **Lord, I believe. Assure me when I doubt, and strengthen my faith. Amen.**

Adam's sin brought guilt, the desire to sin, and mortality to all humans. Praise God, He sent a Second Adam to begin a new humanity. Christ fulfilled the Law. One man—Christ—has redeemed us and changed humanity forever.

❖ **O Lord, Your grace abounds for me so that I may enjoy justification, life, and peace as Adam enjoyed before the fall into sin. Amen.**

Many consider freedom to be the ultimate human right, but no one is truly free spiritually. We were slaves to sin and bound to death. Knowing this, Jesus came to serve us by giving His life on the cross and rising for us. Freed from sin, we can now serve God. Only when we are "slaves" to God will we have freedom to be the people He created us to be.

❖   **My Savior, thank You for serving me. Lead me to serve You and others. Amen.**

We know God's will and desire to serve Him, but we cannot overcome sin. Even if we try, we fail. We cry out, "Who will deliver me from this body of death?" There is only one answer: "Thanks be to God through Jesus Christ our Lord!" Jesus rescues us. Though we sin daily, He continues to forgive and restore us.

✝ **Lord Jesus, lead me in daily repentance. Forgive my sin and strengthen my faith. By Your Spirit, deliver me. Amen.**

Christ's death, resurrection, and exaltation at God's right hand guarantee our victory over anything and everything that would separate us from His love. When following Christ brings distress, we sometimes distance ourselves from Him. But Christ never draws back from us.

❖ **Lord Jesus, though You are exalted at the Father's right hand, You still hold us. Keep us in Your love to the end. Amen.**

In ways beyond our understanding, God has acted in mercy to bring salvation to Jews and Gentiles. Human beings cannot exchange roles with God, presuming to sit in judgment of Him. But we in whom His Spirit dwells praise Him for His inexhaustible kindness toward us in Christ Jesus.

✣　**To You alone, O triune Lord, belongs all glory forever. Amen.**

God graciously bestows various gifts to be used for the benefit of others. Our abilities can cause us to think of ourselves too highly. Paul urges Christians to avoid that temptation while exhorting us to use God's gifts to serve others. Paul repeatedly emphasizes the gracious gifts of God that are received in faith.

❖ **Thank You, God, for the gifts You give to those who have served me in many and various ways. Amen.**

_____

_____

_____

_____

_____

_____

_____

_____

_____

_____

_____

_____

_____

_____

_____

_____

_____

_____

_____

We should not engage in behaviors that would cause other believers to stumble in their faith. When we commit actions against our own Spirit-informed Christian conscience, we sin. Freedom in Christ is not simply freedom from the Law, but freedom given for a purpose, to serve others in love (Galatians 5:13).

❖   **Father, show me when I ought to limit my freedom for the benefit of my brothers and sisters in the faith. Amen.**

God's eternal being, His wisdom, knowledge, and power, are all far beyond ours. He calls those of faith to respond in obedience to His will. The Gospel of Jesus Christ was entrusted to Paul and faithfully proclaimed among the nations in accordance with God's will.

❖   **Lord, use me and the gifts You have given to me as an acceptable offering to You. Amen.**

_____

_____

_____

_____

_____

_____

_____

_____

_____

_____

_____

_____

_____

_____

_____

_____

_____

_____

_____

_____

_____

The message of the cross is simple, but the spiritual wisdom that comes with it touches every area of life and faith. In view of this, we see unbelievers with new compassion, as people with no true spiritual comprehension. The Holy Spirit grants such understanding only through the Gospel.

❖ **Enlighten us with spiritual insight, Holy Spirit. Strengthen us to share Your Word. Amen.**

_____

_____

_____

_____

_____

_____

_____

_____

_____

_____

_____

_____

_____

_____

_____

_____

_____

_____

_____

_____

There is no ground for pride in human achievement in Christ's Church. Such an attitude undermines the very nature of His gifts of salvation and service. God accomplishes everything, living in us by His Spirit.

❖   **"O Holy Spirit, enter in, and in our hearts Your work begin, Your dwelling place now make us." Amen.** (*LSB* 913:1)

_____

_____

_____

_____

_____

_____

_____

_____

_____

_____

_____

_____

_____

_____

_____

_____

_____

_____

_____

_____

_____

_____

Because Christ has united us with Him and with one another, immorality has no place among us. Freedom to live in Christ excludes living in opposition to Him. When we fall into sin, we can repent of the disunity we have brought. Jesus Christ will restore and renew us as His very own.

❖   **Father, be glorified in our freedom, which You grant us in Jesus. Amen.**

Marriage brings obligations, but being in Christ forms a new being. Treasure marriage because of the blessings God provides through it. In marriage, Christians can encourage one another, non-Christians may be drawn to belief, and children can be brought up in the faith.

❖ **God, I thank You for this most precious vestige of the perfection You gave our first parents. Preserve me faithfully according to Your love and Your gifts. Amen.**

_____

_____

_____

_____

_____

_____

_____

_____

_____

_____

_____

_____

_____

_____

_____

_____

_____

_____

_____

_____

_____

_____

_____

_____

Faith is not a private matter. Faithful Christians will be zealous to pray for and carry out God's will that all be saved and come to the knowledge of the truth (1 Timothy 2:3–4). How marvelously our Savior bears with our weaknesses! Most important, He took away our sin and builds us up in love.

❖   **O Lord, stir us up to worship and honor You alone, and through Your Spirit use us to turn others to You. Amen.**

If we participated in churches that do not faithfully confess the Gospel in all its purity, this would indicate that we assent to what that worshiping community believes. For this reason, we avoid such false worship. At the Lord's Table, He offers His body and blood for the forgiveness of sins and through them creates a faithful community.

✣ **From being led astray by the many gods of this world, protect us by Your Spirit, Lord. Amen.**

_____

_____

_____

_____

_____

_____

_____

_____

_____

_____

_____

_____

_____

_____

_____

_____

_____

_____

_____

_____

_____

The sin of arrogance plaguing the Corinthians still disrupts congregations today when roles of service are not clearly defined or valued. Yet also today, Christ unites us in Baptism and makes us His very Body. Though wounded and afflicted, His Body can never be destroyed but carries out God's loving purposes.

❖   **Grant me refuge, dear Jesus, in Your holy wounds, from which You poured life and blessing for me and for all. Amen.**

Paul sharply rebukes all noisy, clanging boasts of superiority. Yet, he alludes to the fact that the Father—who knows His children all too well—still loves them, reaches for them by His Word, and will embrace them eternally because of Christ, who delivered Himself up for us all.

❖ **O Father, when my brothers and sisters disappoint and annoy me, take my hands and stretch them wide to embrace them with Your all-embracing love. Amen.**

The body—corrupted by sin—declines, decays, and dies. Humanly speaking, we can extend our lives only by having children, whom we likewise corrupt with our inherited sin. But thanks be to God! He chose to establish a new order for us through Jesus' life, death, and resurrection. Jesus resisted all corruption and grants us His heavenly life.

✢ **Jesus, lead me to respect my body and to regard my funeral like a farmer sowing with resurrection hope. Amen.**

No matter how or where you serve the Lord, you are part of a larger team. Respect your fellow workers by listening to them and coordinating efforts with them. Our Savior's strong, firm love and leadership preserves the unity of His dear Church, for which He gave His life.

✤ **Dear Jesus, grant me patience with my colleagues, and direct us ever by Your pure Word so that we may stand firm together by Your grace alone. Amen.**

As Christians, we often feel the very real weight of representing Christ to others. Our worries, sins, and frailties can overwhelm us. We can take heart that Christ Jesus is always sufficient and that His message of forgiveness for us is also a sweet fragrance to all who trust in Him.

✠   **Dear Lord, give us sincere hearts to look honestly at ourselves, so we may never take Your grace for granted. Amen.**

God's promises of life and salvation are the most real things in our lives. Because that is true, believers can look at afflictions and struggles purposefully as opportunities that make God's power more evident to those around them. Afflictions are temporary nuisances that will surely give way to the glory of life eternal with our Savior.

❖ **Lord, show me Your purpose in the struggles and in the victories of my life. Amen.**

_____

_____

_____

_____

_____

_____

_____

_____

_____

_____

_____

_____

_____

_____

_____

_____

_____

_____

_____

Too often we mute the Gospel's power because of our pride, our carelessness, or our lack of concern for others. No greater honor can be given us than to be His ambassadors, His spokespeople. He not only saves us but also works through us.

❖ **Dear Lord, continue to deepen our understanding of Your great reconciliation of the world in Christ so we might heartily revel in it with others. Amen.**

We Christians are often guilty of hoarding Christ's great love, rather than making room in our hearts for others. God has loved us with an everlasting love through Jesus Christ. To open up our hearts to others, to let them know of Christ's love, is to experience again the joy of that great love of God for all.

✤   **Lord, teach us daily how great, how long, how wide, and how deep is Your love for every person in this world. Amen.**

_____

_____

_____

_____

_____

_____

_____

_____

_____

_____

_____

_____

_____

_____

_____

_____

_____

_____

_____

_____

Seeing things in an earthly, me-first way is miserly and petty. Instead, we should open our hands to receive from God and extend them to give to our neighbor. We marvel that in Jesus it is always more and never less and rejoice that God's gifts multiply as we receive and share them.

❖   **Lord, open and widen our narrow hearts to You, to Your children, and to all. Amen.**

Believers must wake up to the fact that pure doctrine, right worship, and genuine pastors cannot be taken for granted. Although Christ knew many would cast aside His mercy, He still bore the cross and He still sends out true shepherds with the genuine Gospel.

❖ O Jesus, cause us joyfully to suffer for the sake of remaining connected to You in Your true Church through the service of true shepherds. Amen.

Confident that God's Word will do its work, Paul utters no more stern demand or harsh rebuke. He moves through gentle appeal to end on a triumphant note. We should take our bearings from God's good purpose and the communion of saints. The blessed Trinity is not dry theory but the God of love in whom we have life now and forever.

✤ **Praise to You, Father, Son, and Holy Spirit, that You give Your Church Your very life! Amen.**

Paul presents his core theological argument: justification is by faith in Christ and not by works of the Law. Those who appeal to the Law in addition to Christ as a means of salvation make His death meaningless—worse still, null and void. God's Son loves us and gave Himself for us to free us from the Law's condemnation.

❖ **O God, grant me full confidence in Christ Jesus, who alone can save me. Amen.**

Christ redeems us from the Law's curse by becoming a curse for us. One sin, no matter how trivial it may seem to us, makes us a transgressor of the whole Law and accountable to God (James 2:10). But Christ's death on the cross releases us from the guilt of every transgression.

✤   **O Holy Spirit, continue to strengthen us in the new life of faith begun in our Baptism. Amen.**

The Holy Spirit assures us that we are God's children, redeemed by Jesus Christ and made full heirs of the promise to Abraham. The Spirit never derides God's Son or spiritual matters (1 Corinthians 12:3). Christ earned for us the right to call God "our Father," a prayer taught only by the Spirit.

✤ **Dear Father, in confidence and boldness I bring my needs before You. Hear me for the sake of Jesus alone. Amen.**

DATE

TOPICS

Galatians 5:1–6:18

_____

_____

_____

_____

_____

_____

_____

_____

_____

_____

_____

_____

_____

_____

_____

_____

_____

_____

_____

_____

Christian freedom means walking, conducting oneself, by the Holy Spirit's power and leading. Our sinful flesh, consumed by self-importance, instinctively looks down on others and inevitably causes interpersonal tensions. At Baptism, we were united with Christ, who died to set us free from sin and the way of the Law.

❖ **O Holy Spirit, give us daily victories over sin in our personal life and, above all, the power to love one another. Amen.**

547

Pride tempts us to trust in our commitment to God; doubt makes us worry that we are not committed enough. Jesus blesses us spiritually by leading us to repent of sinful pride by the Law and calming our worried hearts through the Gospel.

✦ **Father, forgive my self-centeredness, and teach me to rely on Your loving plan for me; through Jesus Christ. Amen.**

_____

_____

_____

_____

_____

_____

_____

_____

_____

_____

_____

_____

_____

_____

_____

_____

_____

_____

_____

_____

Judaizers threatened most early Christian communities, teaching that Gentiles had to obey the Old Testament Law in addition to faith in Christ. But Paul insists that God saves both Jews and Gentiles by grace through faith, apart from any works. Today's self-help culture likewise tempts us to try to do it all ourselves.

✢   **Lord, help me to abandon my self-confidence and rejoice in Your grace alone. Amen.**

As Paul considers God's wisdom, grace, and love, he breaks out in prayer and praise. Study of God's Word naturally combines with prayer and praise in the Divine Service, where Christ's gifts are given out, and we receive them with thanksgiving.

✜   **Lord, let these verses be my prayer for my church today. Amen.**

_____

_____

_____

_____

_____

_____

_____

_____

_____

_____

_____

_____

_____

_____

_____

_____

_____

_____

_____

_____

_____

_____

_____

_____

Paul highlights the gifts of Christ that make us His Body; as one Body, we are protected from the dangers of our times. Modern individualism and consumerism make it easy to treat the Church as "all about me." Thanks be to God, the Church is all about Jesus, who provides for our salvation and edification.

❖ **Lord, bind us together by the truth proclaimed by Your faithful ministers. Amen.**

Like the Ephesians, we are confronted every day by a world rebelling against God's way. In our struggle against its temptations, we can rely on Christ's Word and Spirit to lead us.

❖　**Lord, strengthen me to speak and act as You desire. Replace all foul talk from my mouth with praise for You and encouragement for my brothers and sisters in Christ. Amen.**

_____

_____

_____

_____

_____

_____

_____

_____

_____

_____

_____

_____

_____

_____

_____

_____

_____

_____

_____

Paul's imprisonment does not defeat the Gospel, as some had feared. God's wisdom and love so far surpass our abilities that He can and does still bring the truth of the Gospel to light despite all opposition, just as Jesus fulfilled all righteousness and conquered death by His resurrection.

✢   **Almighty and merciful God, forgive our contrary human nature, and give us grace in every situation to hear and pass on the truth and mercy revealed in Your Word. Amen.**

Like Paul, our labor would be meaningless and of no use to others if we lived crookedly and perversely as the world around us lives. But God is at work in us, moving us to hold fast to His Word of life, by which He extends His image and kingdom to others.

❖ **Dear Lord Jesus, please work in us to will and to do Your good pleasure, that we may be blameless in this crooked generation and blameless in the day of Your return. Amen.**

_____

_____

_____

_____

_____

_____

_____

_____

_____

_____

_____

_____

_____

_____

_____

_____

_____

_____

_____

_____

_____

We often focus on earthly comforts, worldly examples of success, and maintaining a youthful appearance for this life. But, while doing this, we starve our souls. Our citizenship is in heaven! Our life is in Christ, who reigns over all things in heaven and earth.

✣ **Dear Lord Jesus, turn us from the destructive ways of our human nature and turn us continually toward the heavenly calling and promises You have set before us. Amen.**

Paul's outpouring of appreciation contrasts sharply with feelings of neglect, resentfulness, and even anger that can arise when we lack the privileges and comforts we expect. Paul invites us to see the blessings and fullness of God that are present in every situation. Christ multiplies those blessings by His grace.

❖ **Dear Lord Jesus, forgive our ingratitude. Turn our minds to dwell on the fullness of life in Your Holy Word. Amen.**

_____

_____

_____

_____

_____

_____

_____

_____

_____

_____

_____

_____

_____

_____

_____

_____

_____

_____

_____

_____

_____

_____

_____

Christians are called to a special form of suffering for the sake of Christ: rejection, ridicule, and persecution. No one likes suffering. Nevertheless, the tears of Christian suffering reflect the glory of the cross of Christ. Remember how God used Christ's sufferings to save us. He will also use our sufferings to bring Christ's saving work to others who have no hope.

❖ **"In suff'ring be Thy love my peace, In weakness be Thy love my pow'r." Amen.** (*LSB* **683:4**)

Eventually, Christless or Christ-lite teachings will separate us from God and from one another. But the treasures of His wisdom and knowledge overcome all temptation and defeat all deception. His words will always encourage us and strengthen us in faith and love.

✤ **Grant, O Lord, that Your Word would be taught in its truth and purity in Christ, and protect us from those who would do otherwise. Amen.**

_____

_____

_____

_____

_____

_____

_____

_____

_____

_____

_____

_____

_____

_____

_____

_____

_____

_____

_____

_____

_____

_____

We do not need to turn to ourselves, to angels, or to anything else for salvation. Jesus is our true God and Savior. This "grocery list" of concluding instructions shows that the Gospel is not an abstract idea. It is the essential truth that transforms individual lives, such as those mentioned here, and continues to transform one person after another.

❖   **Dear Father, thank You for the individuals You use to proclaim to me the Gospel of forgiveness in Christ. Amen.**

Compared to the Thessalonians, we are much poorer in our faith, labor of love, and steadfastness of hope. Even without hardship or persecution, we are slow to confess our faith and live it out in love. Despite our weaknesses and failings, the Lord's unfailing love and forgiveness will sustain us to be His witnesses.

❖ **Lord, make us an exemplary witness for the Gospel, so that Your name may be glorified far beyond our community. Amen.**

_____

_____

_____

_____

_____

_____

_____

_____

_____

_____

_____

_____

_____

_____

_____

_____

_____

_____

_____

_____

_____

_____

We should please God and be faithful to His message rather than speak what is pleasing for people to hear. Let us not make lack of financial resources an excuse. The Lord who commanded His disciples to preach the Gospel to all nations will be with us according to His promise and will enable us to pass through any hardship we may face.

✣ **Help us, Lord, to confess the Gospel of Christ faithfully. Amen.**

Our faith in the Lord and love for one another should be as living and contagious as that of the Thessalonians. The Lord, who has promised to be with us until the end of time, will keep us in His faith and kindle His love in our hearts so that we may love Him and one another.

❖   We praise You, O God, because the gates of hell cannot prevent the sown seed of Your Word from growing. Amen.

Christians grieve over the death of loved ones but not as those who have no hope. The resurrection of our Lord, and the victory we have over death through Him, gives us a living hope, despite the fact that death separates loved ones and causes great pain.

❖ **Thank You, Lord Jesus, for making the way through death a path of hope and joy, due to Your resurrection. Create in our hearts the joy and hope of Your victory over death. Amen.**

Christians should support and encourage one another. We should respect the elders and leaders of our congregations because of their work for the Lord and the whole people of God. The Lord Jesus, by humbling Himself to the point of washing His disciples' feet, showed to us the love He has for all believers.

❖   **Lord, give us Your heart and mind so that our life may be blameless, respecting and loving others. Amen.**

We must set an example to others in what we believe and in what we say and do for them; i.e., by living in faith and in love. Christ is indeed our example, but, much greater and higher than that, He is our Savior!

❖ **Almighty God, we implore You that You would strengthen us through the Lord's Supper in faith toward You and in fervent love toward one another. Amen.**

We should pray for peace for others, even for our enemies. Our prayer for God's peace and grace in our lives is no mere wish. We do have peace with God and with one another through the blood of Christ; by the grace of our Lord, this is a peace that passes all understanding and remains steadfast regardless of external assaults by the devil.

❖ **Lord, I bless You for never having forgotten me and never ceasing to offer me forgiveness anew. Amen.**

_____

_____

_____

_____

_____

_____

_____

_____

_____

_____

_____

_____

_____

_____

_____

_____

_____

_____

_____

If God's desire to save sinners could extend even to Paul, who actively persecuted Jesus' followers, and who is foremost among sinners, then it can certainly extend to us as well. God's mercy and patience for us is demonstrated at the cross, where Jesus died as the substitute for all sinners and won eternal life for all who believe.

❖ **Dear Lord, apply Your Law to our hearts, that we might recognize our sins and be brought to repentance. Amen.**

Our sinful nature may cause us to fail to see that God has given us His divine design for male and female because He loves us and always wants what is for us. Jesus faithfully fulfilled the divine role assigned to Him as the one mediator between God and all people. He willingly submitted Himself to death as the sacred substitute for sinners.

✢ **Blessed Savior, lead us to live out our vocations in submissiveness to You and to Your Word. Amen.**

When given chances to express Jesus' love in deeds of service, it is easy to pass on these opportunities. But, in truth, God calls every Christian to follow His example of self-giving service. Jesus came to serve sinners like us with His forgiveness and salvation (Matthew 20:28). He still serves us today through His means of grace.

❖ **Lord Jesus, inspire us by Your grace joyfully to serve others in Your precious name. Amen.**

God daily and richly provides us with all that we need. To reject God's good gifts, or to receive them thanklessly, is a sin against His graciousness. But God promises His gift of forgiveness to those who turn to Him in repentance and faith. Because of Jesus' sacrificial death for our sins, God does not reject us but receives us as His own children through faith.

❖ **Father, teach us to recognize Your gifts in every realm of life. Lead us always to receive them with thankful hearts. Amen.**

The Church is burdened and liable to be reviled by unbelievers when honor and purity are lacking. Our dear Lord Jesus has made every Christian worthy of eternal honor by His sacrificial death and resurrection. Through faith in Him, even dishonorable sinners are regarded as God's pure and beloved children.

❖ **Lord Jesus, may we selflessly give honor and care to those whom You have given us to love and cherish. Amen.**

As our Savior tenderly cares for us through His Word of promise, we are able to enjoy lives of godliness with contentment. All that we can take with us when we leave this world is the life and immortality that Jesus has given us through faith—and that is more than enough!

✤ Give us grace, dear Lord, rightly to regard the wealth we call our own, that it might not be a curse in our lives but a blessing. Amen.

Exhorting Timothy never to be ashamed of the faith he has been given, Paul exults in the promise of Christ, for whose sake he is imprisoned. Instead of feeling self-conscious about being Christian, we must share in Paul's forthright confession: "I am not ashamed, for I know whom I have believed" (v 12). Our Lord Jesus Christ shall never let us go.

✣   **Thank You, Lord Jesus, that You never leave me or forsake me. Amen.**

When God's Word is front and center in our minds and on our tongues, it acts powerfully to create ongoing repentance and faith. By giving His gift of repentance to us through His Word, our Lord Jesus Christ snatches us from "the snare of the devil."

❖ **Guard my tongue, O Lord, that it may be an instrument of Your praise. Amen.**

Timothy faces a difficult task, but he does not face it alone. God has likewise given fellow Christians to us, whom we will find gathered with us in worship. Partaking of the Word and the Sacraments in the communion of saints, our gracious heavenly Father will lighten our loads and lift our burdens.

❖ **Thank You, Lord, for my fellow Christians whom I name before You in my prayers. Amen.**

God saves us from sin and condemnation and makes us fit for His kingdom. The only logical response to such love, grace, and generosity is, like Paul, to overflow with His praises and share this joyous news with others. Through Jesus Christ, the Father rescues us from our shortcomings yesterday, today, and tomorrow.

❖   **O God, make me a sincere and faithful child in the communion of saints. Amen.**

Our lifestyle, relationships, and behavior must not discredit the Gospel. This sets a very high bar, indeed, and one that we cannot reach without a lot of help. However, God trains us for the present time and gives us hope for the future. He redeems and purifies us to make us His children.

✢ **Jesus, adorn my life with works and confession worthy of the Gospel. Amen.**

We are committed and fervent in our beliefs, but we also check ourselves, our words, and our behavior against God's trustworthy Scripture. We pay attention to the guidance, counsel, and teaching of our pastor and elders.

✤ **O God, Your Word and Sacraments sustain, guide, and nurture me in the one true faith. Guard me against all error. Amen.**

_____

_____

_____

_____

_____

_____

_____

_____

_____

_____

_____

_____

_____

_____

_____

_____

_____

_____

_____

_____

Focus on Jesus should be present in our own friendships and greetings, both with other Christians and with those who do not yet know the Lord. We have opportunities to introduce people to our Lord and Savior. The Lord's grace and peace will strengthen our faith and equip us.

❖ **Lord, I thank You for my friends, and I pray for an opportunity to share Christ with those who have yet to meet You. Amen.**

Although Jesus is heavenly like the angels, He is no mere creature. He is the firstborn Son of the Father, who shares with us all that the Father has. He frees us to receive God's ministry, including the ministry given through the angels.

❖   **Lord Jesus, thank You for creating and sustaining me. By Your Word, keep me in true faith, that I may inherit salvation. Amen.**

Jesus serves as our High Priest to intercede for us before the Father. Without a Savior, we would live in slavery to the fear of death. But Jesus has taken the consequence of our sin and removes our fear. Knowing our weaknesses, He will always help us when we are tempted.

✤ **Lord Jesus, help me always to turn away from sin and to put all my trust in You. Amen.**

Though Moses was a faithful servant in God's household, Jesus is the faithful Son. Since Jesus calls you to your heavenly home, you can be confident that you will share in God's glory. However, beware not to boast of your own faithfulness. Only God is holy and righteous. In Christ, you freely share in God's holiness. He is calling you to glory.

✣ **Lord Jesus, Son of the Father, fill me with Your Spirit of faithfulness. Amen.**

God's people missed rest in the Promised Land through their unbelief. This is a warning to us. God calls us to trust Him and to enter into the rest that He has enjoyed since the completion of creation. In Christ Jesus, we have rest from the accusation of the Law. The Holy Spirit leads us to trust in Christ, granting us everlasting peace.

❖ **Lord Jesus, You are my rest. May I always look to You when I am weary and afraid. Amen.**

If we fail to be fruitful in love, mercy, and generosity, we become like thorns and thistles, fit only for His fire. However, we can be confident that God, who has given us the gift of salvation, will grow the fruit of the Spirit in our lives.

❖ **Come, Holy Spirit. Renew my trust in Jesus, and grow Your fruit in my life. Amen.**

_____

_____

_____

_____

_____

_____

_____

_____

_____

_____

_____

_____

_____

_____

_____

_____

_____

_____

_____

_____

_____

If we doubt God's Word, we act as if God were a liar and miss the blessings that flow from a trusting relationship with Him. As we trust God's promises, we see that God tells the truth, and we share in the blessings of eternal life.

❖ **Lord God, I will trust Your Word and receive what You graciously give. Amen.**

In Jesus we have access to God's blessings. His perfect work reminds us that death will always cut short even the best effort that anyone makes to serve God. However, Jesus freely brings us God's eternal blessings through His sacrificial death.

❖ **Father, thank You for providing us with a true High Priest, who serves us with purity and perfection. Amen.**

The old covenant, because it could not permanently address the problem of sin, would "vanish away." As Priest, Christ came to establish an everlasting covenant and atonement for our sins.

✣　O merciful God, forgive us our sins for the sake of Jesus' sacrifice. Amen.

Christ will come from His heavenly sanctuary and take us to Himself with joy. Our greatest joy should be Jesus and His priestly ministry, for He delighted in us, making us the heirs of His last will and testament.

❖   **Lord Jesus, by Your blood there is forgiveness of sins. Continue to purify me that I might honor You. Amen.**

Christ offered up only one sacrifice for the sins of the world—Himself. He "perfects" or completes us by applying the benefits of His sacrifice to us in Holy Baptism and in His Holy Supper. Whenever you study the Word or hear it at church, expect the Lord to change your life and strengthen your faith, for He desires to change your heart and mind by grace.

✢ **Merciful God, for Jesus' sake forgive my sins. Grant me the Holy Spirit, that I may fulfill Your will. Amen.**

All Christians need patience through many sorrows. God calls us to do His will, bearing our crosses patiently, and He equips us with His Word and Spirit. He has promised eternal salvation to all who steadfastly confess Christ.

❖ **Lord Jesus, strengthen me to confess You without wavering. When I fall, grant me a repentant heart. Amen.**

Faith trusts even without sight what God has set forth in His Word. True faith is active in love and is steadfast under persecution. By His resurrection, Christ conquered death and now provides His Holy Spirit to strengthen us.

✤ "Lord, be our light when worldly darkness veils us; Lord, be our shield when earthly armor fails us; And in the day when hell itself assails us, Grant us Your peace, Lord." Amen. (*LSB* 659:3)

God sees you as holy through Christ's sacrifice and disciplines you to struggle against sin. The unpleasant discipline shows that the Lord loves you as a true child. Put your faith into practice by encouraging others and by doing works of service. The Lord is ever serving you, granting repentance, taking away your sins, and equipping you for a godly life.

❖ **Heavenly Father, share with me Your holiness, and let me see You face-to-face eternally. Amen.**

Hebrews sets forth God's grace in Christ, earned on the cross, ratified in the new covenant, and distributed in Word and Sacrament. By holding fast to the teaching of this sermon and by receiving God's grace through faith, we have fellowship with the writer of Hebrews and all the saints and look forward to our inheritance with them in heaven.

✣ **Grant us grace, O Lord, to bear all the crosses of this life. Bring us, with all the saints, into the heavenly city. Amen.**

James encourages Christians to return to the Word, take comfort in the Gospel, and live righteous lives focused on service toward others. We know the kind of lives God calls us to lead. Yet too easily we turn away from that calling. God, who implanted His Word in us and justified us in Christ, now calls us to bless others.

✢ **Lord, may Your Word be rooted deep inside me, that it may transform me into Your righteous servant. Amen.**

_____

_____

_____

_____

_____

_____

_____

_____

_____

_____

_____

_____

_____

_____

_____

_____

_____

_____

_____

_____

True faith and its response of true good works cannot be separated. Works naturally follow faith. God has given us a great gift—through Christ Jesus, He has forgiven us and declared us righteous and holy. He now blesses us by calling us to serve Him in the lives of those around us. A living faith leads us to gladly share with others what we have freely received in Christ.

✤ **By Your Spirit, grant me true faith, Lord, that Your name might be glorified through me. Amen.**

Christians struggle with sins and are even tempted to present themselves as holier than others. How different is the wisdom of God! He has purified us in Christ and freed us from the stain of the world. We now walk in the works He has prepared for us to do.

❖   **O Lord, use my lips to speak Your glory, to tell of Your wonderful deeds, and to proclaim Your salvation. Amen.**

James reminds us to seek what "the Lord wills." This simple statement is a confession of faith and shows confidence in the Lord's care for us. Time and again, He has shown His fatherly, divine goodness and mercy toward us. He has given us life by His Son, Jesus Christ. Now, freed from seeking our own needs, we serve others.

✢ **Thank You, Lord, for the gift of each day. Help me to see each one as guided by Your care and lived for Your glory. Amen.**

We hide behind facades of perfection, but sin and its consequences pervade every aspect of our lives. Left on our own, we would perish. But our Lord has given us a community of fellow saints to hear our confession, pray for our needs, and restore us when we err. As His people, healed in body and soul, we may approach His throne of grace with confidence.

❖ **Lord, use my voice to praise You, to pray for my brothers and sisters, and to speak Your forgiving Word. Amen.**

_____

_____

_____

_____

_____

_____

_____

_____

_____

_____

_____

_____

_____

_____

_____

_____

_____

_____

_____

_____

_____

Even before creation, God knew that mankind would fall into sin. In His love, before the world was made, He determined to send His Son, the unblemished Lamb, to be our sacrifice. He was willing to send His Son for us. Now He calls us to share the Savior with others.

✣ **Heavenly Father, thank You for the gift of Your Gospel, that through Your Son we are born again, forgiven, and given life everlasting. Amen.**

Scripture never teaches that those who follow Jesus will be immune to suffering. Just as Jesus, our sinless Savior, faced unjust suffering and death, so we may be called to take up our own cross to follow Him. But if God gives us a cross to carry, He also promises to give us the strength to bear it by faith.

❖　Gracious God, we praise You for Your mercy through Your Son, who bore our sins in His body on the tree. Amen.

_____

_____

_____

_____

_____

_____

_____

_____

_____

_____

_____

_____

_____

_____

_____

_____

_____

_____

_____

_____

God permits suffering in our lives for a variety of reasons. Sometimes it comes as a direct result of our own sin in order to discipline us. Other times it is an effect of being God's child in a world that wants to crush His Church. Although we do not know God's hidden will, we trust He has only the best in mind for us.

✣   **Lord God, in the midst of trials and persecution, keep our hearts and minds stayed on You, our only refuge. Amen.**

Jesus suffered for us at the hands of evil men. Yet He trusted in His Father with unswerving faith. Whatever trials or difficulties we may face, we can likewise rely on the true grace of God and on the bond of love in our Christian family. Through Jesus, we truly have peace.

✣   **Lord Jesus, may we always rely on Your Word and Your strength, that we may confidently believe in You and always follow Your ways. Amen.**

_____

_____

_____

_____

_____

_____

_____

_____

_____

_____

_____

_____

_____

_____

_____

_____

_____

_____

_____

_____

Peter affirms the greatness of the Christian hope, and he encourages his readers to make their calling and election sure by giving evidence of their faith with good works. We are saved by faith alone, but faith is never alone. In spite of our many failures to bear God-pleasing fruit, our Lord strengthens us daily through Holy Baptism.

✣ **O Lord, thank You that by Your grace there will be richly provided for us an entrance into Your eternal kingdom. Amen.**

Do we use the time allotted to us to take sin and salvation seriously, or do we neglect our worship and prayers and our Lord's gracious call to repent? Make daily repentance part of your life. The patient Lord is ever working through Word and Sacrament to restore fallen sinners and to strengthen them in the stability of their salvation.

✛ O Lord, strengthen me through Your Word, that I may grow in Your grace and proclaim Your glory forever. Amen.

Our sinful pride rejects God's Word and seeks to deceive us so that we might not know ourselves as we are or know God as He has revealed Himself. God sees our true nature, and in Christ He reveals His nature, which is both just and gracious to us.

✣   **Heavenly Father, give us hearts to believe and to know ourselves as we are. Then we may truthfully confess our sins, trusting in Your forgiveness and mercy. Amen.**

There are many antichrists, false teachers who infiltrate the Church and attempt to draw Christians away from the true Christ. There is great danger for us if we do not know the Scriptures well and are unable to recognize false teachers. In God's Word and by His Spirit, we have everything we need to tell the difference between the truth and a lie.

✤ **Heavenly Father, keep us steadfast in Your Word, and ever guard us from the deceptions of the many antichrists. Amen.**

We are often tempted to rationalize and excuse our sin. Those who give themselves over to sin will not be exonerated by the excuses they put forward. Through daily repentance and the practice of righteousness, we show ourselves to be true children of God and will not be ashamed when our Lord Jesus appears on the Last Day.

❖ **Father, forgive my sinful excuses so I may remain in Christ through Your Word and love as He has loved me. Amen.**

DATE

TOPICS

1 John 4:1–21

As long as we remain in fellowship with the Father through faith, we love one another and have no fear of Judgment Day. Whenever we do not treat our brother with love as Jesus has loved us, we fear God's punishment. Because He sent His Son to take away our sins, we gain confidence to stand before God without fear.

❖ **Heavenly Father, forgive me and work Your love in me to cast out my fear of punishment. Amen.**

All wrongdoing is sin, and any sin could lead to death if not for the Righteous One, Jesus Christ, who cleanses us from all sin by His blood. Not only can we be confident of our own forgiveness in Him who is the genuine Savior and the true God, but we can also be certain that God desires our repentance and life because of Jesus.

✤ **Son of God, protect us from the evil one, and keep us from every idol. Amen.**

The apostle is planning to come and set straight all outstanding issues. Until then, the congregation has his warning and admonition to stand firm in the faith. You, too, have the apostle's testimony and all of Holy Scripture. Abide in God's revelation and beware of strange teachings that diminish the person and work of Jesus, who is your salvation and joy.

❖ **Lord, grant us to remain faithful to Your teaching. Amen.**

_____

_____

_____

_____

_____

_____

_____

_____

_____

_____

_____

_____

_____

_____

_____

_____

_____

_____

_____

_____

_____

Whatever flattery or intimidation people may use to get their way, there always comes a day when they will be shamed before God and His faithful. God will bring their threats and accusations into the light. Trust the Lord to protect you when you support the truth. He will deliver you by His Son, who is "the way, and the truth, and the life" (John 14:6).

❖   **Heavenly Father, give us courage to stand up against the plots of those who would harm our congregation. Amen.**

Christians, who have the full salvation already delivered to them in Scripture, need not fall into deceptions. We have been warned about false teaching and the deception of sin that leads to death. Likewise, the Lord has taught us the path of righteousness by which His Spirit leads us in the Gospel of grace and peace.

❖ **Lord God, keep us in Your love and mercy in Christ until He comes to deliver us from all evil. Amen.**

_____

_____

_____

_____

_____

_____

_____

_____

_____

_____

_____

_____

_____

_____

_____

_____

_____

_____

_____

_____

John instinctively falls down before Jesus, trembling with fear. We would surely react the same way in His presence. But Jesus is not merely about overwhelming power and glory. He was made like us in every way except without sin. Having overcome death and the grave, He now promises to share His eternal life and glory with us.

❖ "Oh come, let us worship and bow down; let us kneel before the Lord, our Maker!" (Psalm 95:6). Amen.

The Thyatirans must avoid idolatrous worship and sexual immorality. We, too, must remain vigilant against such failures and repent of the times we have fallen short. By God's grace, we remain faithful to the Word of Christ and so share with Him in ruling His eternal kingdom.

✤ **Deliver us, dear Savior, from the deceptive doctrines and practices of this present age and prepare us for the age to come. Amen.**

Becoming complacent and self-satisfied about our Christian walk can be as destructive as outright hostility and persecution. Despite this common failing, Christ still comes to us in His Word and Sacrament, granting repentance and forgiveness. He calls us to follow Him into life everlasting.

❖ "O mighty Rock, O Source of life, Let Your dear Word, in doubt and strife, In us be strongly burning." Amen. (*LSB* 913:3)

The character of heavenly worship powerfully underscores the glory of Christ's redeeming work. Apart from Him, our fallen world has no hope. However, because Jesus was slain and then conquered death, His people are ransomed and have the hope of glory.

❖ **"Worthy is Christ, the Lamb who was slain, whose blood set us free to be people of God. . . . Blessing, honor, glory and might be to God and the Lamb forever." Amen.** (*LSB*, p 155)

_____

_____

_____

_____

_____

_____

_____

_____

_____

_____

_____

_____

_____

_____

_____

_____

_____

_____

_____

John depicts the end times with successive trumpet blasts. The visions are frightful, since we all know in our hearts that we cannot stand before God in the judgment. Fortunately, we have one who stands beside us as our advocate—Jesus Christ. His blood cleanses us from all unrighteousness.

✣ "Bold shall I stand in that great day, Cleansed and redeemed, no debt to pay; Fully absolved through these I am From sin and fear, from guilt and shame." Amen. (*LSB* **563:2**)

"Take up the shield of faith, with which you can extinguish all the flaming darts of the evil one" (Ephesians 6:16). Because our sworn enemy is so cunning and powerful, it is comforting to hear that Christ has already overcome him and will defeat him once and for all on the Last Day.

✠   **"O Thou, whose coming is with dread To judge the living and the dead, Preserve us from the ancient foe While still we dwell on earth below." Amen. (*LSB* 351:5)**

John describes his prophetic commissioning. On the one hand, the content of John's prophecy is bitter, for it reveals God's wrath against a hostile world. On the other hand, the Word he brings from God is the sweetest possible message, for it delivers Jesus' salvation to many peoples.

❖　**Lord God, I recognize that I fully deserve Your punishment. Nevertheless, Christ assures me in the sweet Gospel that He has paid for my sins and removed all judgment from me. Amen.**

For now, people can refuse to obey God. But such resistance will someday be met with an irresistible outpouring of wrath and judgment. Christ's people need not fear that day. Instead, they may long for the day when God will be all in all, and perfect harmony will again prevail.

✜ **"And when the fight is fierce, the warfare long, Steals on the ear the distant triumph song, And hearts are brave again, and arms are strong. Alleluia! Alleluia!" Amen. (*LSB* 677:5)**

_____

_____

_____

_____

_____

_____

_____

_____

_____

_____

_____

_____

_____

_____

_____

_____

_____

_____

_____

_____

_____

Although Satan cannot overcome the Church, he nonetheless tries his hardest to drag down with him as many as possible. It is most comforting to know, therefore, that Jesus has already defeated Satan and forgiven our sins, so that we can never be lost.

❖   **We thank You, Lord God, for giving us the victory over the devil through Your Son, Jesus. Amen.**

Have we ever allowed an authority besides God to determine what is right or wrong for us? Have we ever obeyed man rather than God? If so, seek God's forgiveness in Christ. He invites us to believe that He chose us and wrote our name in His Book of Life before the world began.

❖   **Father, I thank You for making me Your own child through Christ Jesus. Grant me strength always to endure even difficult days, especially in these last times before the end. Amen.**

John relates a vision of three angels warning the world against the disaster that will come upon those worshiping the beast. Despite such admonitions, people, including those who know better, still chase after false gods. Those who remain faithful to God and His Word will be blessed, however, entering into eternal rest when they pass out of this world.

❖   **God, continue giving me strength to withstand all enticements to abandon the faith. Amen.**

This vision is how things typically are: the most sublime moments of rejoicing are followed by dreadful calamities, and hope is ever threatened by evil and judgment. Given this sad state of affairs, the Church needs to hear over and over again that there is "now no condemnation for those who are in Christ Jesus" (Romans 8:1).

✛   **Heavenly Father, thank You for making us Your people and so removing from us any fear of the impending wrath. Amen.**

Peter poses a question we all need to consider daily: what sort of people ought we to be (2 Peter 3:11)? The only basis for confidence on Judgment Day is that our Lord Jesus paid the full price of our punishment while dying on the cross (John 19:30), then rose from the dead and returned to the Father, where even now He is preparing a place for us.

❖　**Lord, receive our heartfelt thanks for having Jesus bear Your judgment for us. Amen.**

Earthly power structures, when built upon idolatrous worldviews and characterized by ungodly ambitions, are not morally neutral but rather stand in opposition to God and His Church. In the end, however, the King of kings and Lord of lords will get the victory and share it with the faithful, so that they reign with Him eternally.

❖ **Lord, give us sound judgment in all things, so that we may remain faithful and enter with You into glory! Amen.**

As we hear the charges against Babylon, some strike very close to home, especially greed and an addiction to luxury. The Church must remember where its true treasures are to be found. Whoever has Jesus can look forward to enjoying eternal splendor and joy in heaven.

✤ **Lord Jesus, help us to be responsible stewards of the wealth and gifts that You entrust to us, for Jesus' sake. Amen.**

Christ returns and begins to destroy the remaining enemies of His rule once and for all. The end of those who oppose God and His Messiah is fearful, as birds of prey will devour their flesh. But the faithful know that Jesus will come to right wrong and redress evil, and that He freely pardons all who embrace His mercy.

❖ **Lord, grant to all people true repentance and sincere faith, so that we may all enter with You into eternal bliss. Amen.**

Since our first parents fled from the Lord in the garden (Genesis 3:24), all their sinful descendants have been shutting their eyes and ears to the somber truth about the last judgment (cf. Hebrews 10:31). However, Christ has covered us in the mantle of His righteousness. Consequently, our bodily resurrection will be unto glory and eternal bliss in God's presence.

❖ **Lord Jesus, grant us always to look to You for deliverance from the powers of hell. Amen.**

The climax of this Book and indeed all of history at last comes clear: the restored heaven and earth is presented to God's resurrected people. God is faithful and so will unfailingly fulfill the purposes for which His Son became man; He will remove the curse that so sorely afflicts us.

❖ **Jesus, renew our hearts and minds, and hasten the day when You shall present the holy city as Your beloved Bride, the Church. Amen.**

Revelation shows how infinitely greater God is than evil. By offering a vision of the new creation soon to be revealed, Revelation draws us on toward our blessed hope in Christ. To Him be power and glory throughout the ages!

✣   **Blessed Redeemer, help us to keep these holy words and thereby conquer sin, death, and the devil. Amen.**

PERSONAL INDEX

ABANDONMENT
Ps 88–89:8

ADOPTION
Ps 68:4–6; Eph 1:5

ADULTERY
Gn 39:7–10; Heb 13:4

ANGELS
Ps 91:11–12; Lk 2:13

ANGER
Gn 4:6–7; Jn 2:13–17

**ANXIETY/
NERVOUSNESS**
Ps 37; Php 4:6–7

ARMOR OF GOD
Eph 6:10–18

ASSURANCE
Ps 37; Jer 29:11

BAPTISM
Mt 29:19–20; Gal
3:26–27

BEATITUDES
Mt 5:1–12

BETRAYAL
Ps 41

BLESSINGS
Ps 145:14–16; 1Tm
4:4–5

**BODY OF CHRIST
(THE CHURCH)**
1Co 12:12–31

CHANGES
Is 40:6–8; Heb 13:8

CHILDREN
Dt 11:18–21; Mk
10:13–16

COMPASSION
Ex 22:27; Mt 9:36

COMPLAINING
Nu 14

CONFESSION
Ps 51

CONFLICT
Mt 10:34–39

CONTENTMENT
Ps 63; Php 4:11–13

COURAGE
Jsh 1:1–9; 2Co 5:6–8

COVETOUSNESS
1Ki 21; Lk 12:13–21

CREATION
Gn 1–2; Col 1:16

DEATH
Ps 23; 1Th 4:13–18

DEBT
Mt 6:19–34

DECEPTION
Ps 55; Pr 6:12–19

DEPRESSION
1Pt 5:8–9

DISCIPLES
Mt 28:19–20

DISCIPLESHIP
Mk 8:34–9:1

DISCIPLINE
Heb 12:5–11

DIVORCE
Mt 19:1–12; 1Co 7

DOUBT
Ps 13; 73; Jn 20:24–29

DRUNKENNESS
Rm 13:11–14

EDUCATION
Pr 1:2–8

ELDERLY
Lv 19:32

ELDERS
Nu 11:16–30

ELECTION, DIVINE
Rm 9–11

ENCOURAGEMENT
Ps 91; Col 4:2–6

END TIMES
Lk 13:22–14:24

ENVY
Ps 73; Rm 1:28–32

ETERNAL LIFE
Jn 3:16

EVANGELISM
Ac 22:30–23:11

EVIL
2Tm 4:18

EVOLUTION
Heb 11:3

FAITH
Rm 4; 10:17; Heb 11

FALSE PROPHETS
Mt 24:23–24

FELLOWSHIP
Ac 2:42–47

FOLLOWING GOD
Mt 4:18–22; 16:24–28

FORGIVENESS
Ps 51; 130; Mt 6:14–15

FRIENDS/FRIENDSHIP
1Sm 18:1–5

FUTURE
Ps 139; Mt 6:34; 24:36

GENEROSITY
Mt 5:40–42

GENTLENESS
1Tm 6:11

GIVING
Mt 6:1–4; 2Co 9:7

GOD
Is 63:16 1Jn 4:8

GOOD WORKS
Gal 2:15–3:296

GOSPEL
Jn 3:16, Rm 1:16

GOSSIP
Pr 6:12; 16:28

GOVERNMENT
Rm 13; Mt 22:21

GRACE
Eph 2:1–10

GREAT COMMANDMENT
Mt 22:34–40

GREAT COMMISSION
Mt 28:16–20

GREED
Lk 12:13–15; 16:1–13

GRIEF
Jn 11:1–44; 2Co 1:3–7

GUILT
Ps 51; Heb 12:1–2

HAPPINESS
Jn 15:11

HATRED
Lv 19:17; 1Jn 2:9–11

HEALTH
2Co 4:16–5:9

HEAVEN
Rv 22:3–5

HELL
Mt 24:51

HERESY
2Pt 2:1

HEROES
Heb 11

HOMOSEXUALITY
Lv 18:22; 1Co 6:9–10

HONESTY
Pr 24:23–34

HOPE
Rm 15:13

HOSPITALITY
Gn 18:4; Rm 12:13

HUMILITY
Mt 18:1–6; Jas 4:10

HYPOCRISY
Mt 23

IDOLATRY
Ex 20:3–6; 1Co 10:1–22

IMAGE OF GOD
Gn 1:26–27

IMMORALITY
Rm 1:18–32; 1Co 6:9–11

INJUSTICE
Gn 39; Am 5:14–15, 21–24;

JESUS CHRIST
Lk 2:1–21; Jn 19:17–37

JOY
Php 4:4

JUDGMENT DAY
Mt 25:1–13, 31–46

JUSTIFICATION
Rm 3:23–26; 4

KINDNESS
Zec 7:9

KNOWING GOD
Gal 4:9

LAST DAYS
Mt 24:36–51; 2Tm 3

LAW
Rm 2:14–15; 3:20

LIES/LYING
Pr 6:12–19; 14:5

LIFE
Psalm 139:16

LONELINESS
Jer 29:11; Ps 88

LORD'S PRAYER
Mt 6:5–14; Lk 11:1–4

LORD'S SUPPER
Lk 22:7–23; 1Co 11:17–34

LOVE
Dt 7:6–13; Jn 3:16; 1Co 13

LOYALTY
Pr 20:6; Mk 3:31–35

LUST
Mt 5:27–28

MARRIAGE
Gn 2:24–25; 1Co 7

MEDITATION
Ps 1

MERCY
Rm 9:18; Ti 3:5–6

MINISTERS
1Co 3–4

MINISTRY
Eph 4:11–16

MISSIONS
Ps 145; 2Th 3:1–5

MONEY
Ec 5:10; 1Tm 6:10

MOURNING
Jb 2:13

MURDER
Gn 4; Rm 1:28–32

MUSIC
Ps 100

NEW LIFE
Rm 6; Eph 4:17–32

OATH
Ex 20:7; Mt 5:33–37

OBEDIENCE
Lv 26; Heb 13:7

OCCULT
1Sm 28; Ec 7:14

OVERWHELMED
Ps 91; 130; Mt 11:28–30

PAIN
Ps 147:3

PARENTS/PARENTING
Pr 22:6; Eph 6:1–4

PASTORS
1Tm 3:1–7

PATIENCE
Ps 27:14

PEACE
Jn 14:27

PEER PRESSURE
Mk 15:6–15

PERSECUTION
Ps 54

PERSEVERANCE
Jude 17–23

POLITICS
Ps 146; Rm 13

POOR
Lv 26:35–46; Jas 2:1–7

POPULARITY
Jn 2:15–17

POSSESSIONS
Lk 12:33

PRAISE
2Ch 5:11–13

PRAYER
Mt 6:5–13

PREACHING
Ac 14:1

PRIDE
Lk 14:7–11

PROMISES
2Co 1:20

PROSPERITY
Jer 29:11

PROTECTION
Ex 14:14; Ps 91

PURITY
Lv 11–15

QUESTIONING GOD
Ps 13

REBELLION
Nu 14, 16

RECONCILIATION
Rm 5

REDEMPTION
Ex 12–13; 1Co 1:30

REJECTION
Ps 118:22; Rm 11:2

REPENTANCE
Ac 3:19–21; 2Pt 3:9

REST
Mt 11:25–30

RESTORATION
Ps 23; 1Pt 5:2

REVENGE
Mt 5:38–42

RIGHTEOUSNESS
Ps 5

RIVALRY
Php 1:15–18

SADNESS
Lk 19:41–44

SALVATION
Mt 1:21; Ac 4:12

SANCTIFICATION
Rm 6; 1Co 1:30; 6:11

SATAN
Jb 1:6–2:10; Mt 4:1–11

SAVIOR
Mt 1:21; Jn 4:42

SCRIPTURE, HOLY
Ps 119; Jn 5:39; 20:31

SECOND COMING
Rv 1:7

SELF-ESTEEM
Ps 139; 2Co 5:17

SELF-EXAMINATION
Mt 7:1–6

SELFISHNESS
Jas 3:13–18

SEXUALITY
Pr 5:15–19; Rm 13:11–14

SEXUAL SIN
Rm 1:24–27; 1Co 6:9–20

SHARING
Gal 6:1–10

SICKNESS
Mt 4:23–24; 8:14–17

SIGNS
Mt 16:1–4

SIN
Ps 51; Mt 15:19

SINGING
Col 3:16

SINGLENESS
1Co 7:25–40

SPIRITUAL GIFTS
1Co 12:1–11

SPIRITUAL GROWTH
Mt 13:1–23

SPIRITUAL WARFARE
Eph 6:10–20

STEADFASTNESS
1Tm 6:11–16; Jas 1:2–18

STEWARDSHIP
Ps 116; 2Co 9

STRESS
Mt 11:28–30

SUBMISSION
Rm 13:1–7; Eph 5:22–24

SUFFERING
Ps 88

TEACHERS
Dt 6:4–9

TEAMWORK
Col 3:18–4:1

TEMPTATION
1Co 10:12–13

TERRORISM
Ps 10

TESTING
Ex 17:1–7; Jas 1

THANKFULNESS
Col 3:16

THANKSGIVING
Ps 18; 136; Php 4:4–7

TRAGEDY
Lk 13:1–5

TRANSGRESSION
Ex 34:6–7

TRUST
Ps 56

UNBELIEF
Jn 11:37–50; Rm 1:18–32

UNCERTAINTY
1Th 1:4–5

UNFAITHFULNESS
Jgs 2:11–15; Jas 4:4–12

UNITY, CHRISTIAN
Ac 4:32–35; Rm 12:9–21

VICTORY
1Co 15:54–56

VIGILANCE
Pr 4:23; Mt 25:1–12

VIOLENCE
Gn 6:11–13

VOCATION
1Co 7:17

WAITING
Lk 12:35–40

WAR
Jsh 5:13–12:24

WEALTH
Mt 19:16–29; Mk 10:17–30

WISDOM
1Ki 3:3–15; Ps 1; 19:8–15

WITNESSING
Mt 5:14–16; Ac 1:6–8

WOMEN
Pr 31:10–31; Lk 8:1–3

WORD OF GOD
Heb 4:12

WORKS RIGHTEOUSNESS
Rm 3:9–31; 11:5–6

WORRYING
Ps 27; 56; Mt 6:25–34

WORSHIP
Ex 4:31; 26; 33:10

YOUTH
Ec 11:9–12:8; Jas 5:5